25 Principles of Service Leadership

by

Po Chung

Co-founder, DHL International, Asia Pacific

Chairman, Hong Kong Institute of Service Leadership & Management

and

Art Bell, PhD

Director, Center for Service Leadership

Clarkson University, New York

25 Principles of Service Leadership

First Edition

ISBN 13 digit: 978-0985948054

ISBN 10 digit: 0985948051

Lexingford Publishing

New York   Hong Kong   San Francisco   Ottawa

www.lexingfordpublishingllc.com

25 Principles of Service Leadership

Preface

The world is waking up to the fact that service in all its myriad forms is a powerful economic and social force—and in many global commercial centers, the most powerful economic and social driver. By "service," we include all those occupations that do not center on the creation of a product. While waiters, hotel staff, and gas station attendants may leap first to mind, service providers also include physicians, lawyers, soldiers, politicians, teachers, stock brokers, and all the other professions that earn their way through service.

Only in the last decade has service education, and particularly education in service leadership, been recognized by secondary and tertiary teachers as a subject "missing-in-action" in the typical curriculum.

Even though the majority of university graduates predictably will not find themselves in product-focused careers, the courses they take continue to emphasize supply chain management, marketing, quality control, and information technology geared to assembly line thinking.

Where in the modern university curriculum or in company training programs do students learn to become service leaders?

In this short book, we offer 25 principles that may serve to define and motivate the education of service leaders, both in a university setting and in their careers. We admit from the outset that there is no magic to the number "25" as applied to these principles. Surely the complex field of service leadership could be teased out to twice that number or, from a 30,000 foot view, condensed down to a dozen principles or less.

In the process of writing, however, we have discovered that for the purposes of a short, readable book the limit of 25 principles gave us room to express the variety of concepts, philosophies, attitudes and behaviors that undergird service leadership without repeating ourselves or skipping important areas.

The organization of each Principle is divided into a succinct statement of "The Concept" followed by a more expansive and reflective stroll through "Commentary," that is, the author's interpretation and elaboration on the central themes within the Principle at hand.

With humility in light of the work yet to be done in service leadership, we nevertheless offer here both our passion and experience in the subject before us. In addition to a lifelong pursuit in learning about the nature of service in all its forms, I, Po Chung, bring to the reader the perspective of having led a major service company, DHL, through its impressive expansion throughout Asia. And I, Art Bell, offer my experience and insight as a scholar of service leadership and Director of Service Leadership at Clarkson University, New York.

25 Principles of Service Leadership

True to our call for active listening as a key attribute for service leaders, we welcome comments and other communication from readers. We are especially eager to learn about your efforts to improve service leadership as a career tool in your own life and a reality in the life of your organization. Please contact us through the publisher at lexingfordpublishing@gmail.com.

Po Chung and Art Bell

Hong Kong

September, 2015

25 Principles of Service Leadership

Acknowledgments from Po Chung

This book was built on the more than four decades of experience I've had as a service leader. I wish to recognize the people who helped me share my experience and insights.

Art Bell, as my editor at Lexingford Publishing, played an invaluable role in helping me find the words by which to best communicate my message here.

I also thank my good friend Tom Osgood, who encouraged me to write this book. He was the one who first parsed my written texts and conversations to narrow down the principles to the 25 described here.

I am also indebted to the generous support from the Victor & William Fung Foundation, who are as committed as I am to the advancement of service leadership training and practice.

Finally, I would like to knowledge the support from the Hong Kong Institute of Service Leadership & Management (HKI-SLAM), which has coordinated the development of materials that falls under the Service Leadership & Management umbrella.

Acknowledgments from Art Bell

I owe a profound intellectual debt to the primary service leaders in my professional life; namely Tony Collins, President of Clarkson University; Chuck Thorpe, Provost; Bill Jemison, Dean of the School of Engineering; Peter Turner, Dean of Arts and Sciences; and Dayle Smith, Dean of the School of Business. I learn from them on a day-to-day basis the practical, ethical strategies that lead an organization forward and convert good intentions into excellent programs. I value these esteemed colleagues as service leaders of the highest order.

I also acknowledge the hundreds of scholars who have written with insight and passion in the areas of customer satisfaction, leadership, team building, organizational development, and managerial communication. They have created a rich reservoir of knowledge and case materials from which this work has arisen. Although the topic of service leadership is relatively new as a defined area of scholarly research and teaching, it is quickly gaining the attention of academia at all levels, spurred in large part by the groundbreaking work of Hong Kong's eight major universities, the thought leadership of the Hong Kong Institute of Service Management led by Po Chung, and the encouragement and support of the Li & Fung Foundation.

Dedication

Po Chung dedicates this work to the future generations of Hong Kong.

He extends his deepest gratitude to his dearest wife, Helen, three daughters, Yana, Anca and Yangie, their son-in-law, Eric, and their grandsons, Connor and Trevor.

Art Bell dedicates his role in this work to his children: Art Jr., Lauren, and Madeleine, all of whom are happily pursuing fulfilling careers in service leadership.

25 Principles of Service Leadership

25 Principles of Service Leadership

Table of Contents

Introduction   13

Principle 1: The Principle of 15 Minutes
of Leadership   23

Principle 2: The Principle of Self-Leadership   27

Principle 3: The Principle of People
Leadership   33

Principle 4: The Principle of the Server   37

Principle 5: The Principle of Competence,
Character, and Caring (the Three C's)   43

Principle 6: The Principle of Co-created
Service Leadership   53

Principle 7: The Principle of Knowing Who
You Are   59

Principle 8: The Principle of Personal Ethics   65

Principle 9: The Principle of Whom You Hire   71

Principle 10: The Principle of Authoritarian
Leadership and Distributed Leadership   77

Principle 11: The Principle of Trust, Fairness,
Respect, and Care   87

Principle 12: The Principle of POS
(Personal Operating System)   93

Principle 13: The Principle of Personal Brand   101

25 Principles of Service Leadership

Principle 14: The Principle of Relationship   107

Principle 15: The Principle of Service   113

Principle 16: The Principle of Mentor-Follower   119

Principle 17: The Principle of Historical Service
Development   125

Principle 18: The Principle of Tradable
and Non-tradable Service   131

Principle 19: The Principle of a Service Mindset 139

Principle 20: The Principle of Transformation and
Inspiration   145

Principle 21: The Principle of Global Extension
of Service Relationships   151

Principle 22: The Principle of Habitat
Management   157

Principle 23: The Principle of the Diaspora
Mindset   163

Principle 24: The Principle of Anna Karenina   169

Principle 25: The Principle of Wrapped Service
(The Hamburger Principle)   177

Resources: Further Learning in Service
Leadership   185

25 Principles of Service Leadership

Introduction

There's no mystery here.

You *know* when you receive excellent service, whether by a sales clerk or a highly paid professional such as a lawyer, physician, or financial advisor. In fact, you probably tell others about your good experience: how the person not only met your expectations but exceeded them, with a caring attitude that encouraged an on-going business or professional relationship.

On the flip side, you also know instinctively when you have been ill-served. The causes can be myriad: perhaps the server didn't know his job; he may not have understood what you wanted; he may have given unwarranted priority to others over you; he may have allowed negative emotions from other parts of his life to influence his interaction with you; or, he may simply not have cared.

But one thing is for sure. You told plenty of people—perhaps dozens over a period of time—about your experience with poor service. You told them not only what happened (often in animated detail), but also how you *felt*.

25 Principles of Service Leadership

Your bad experience with a particular service provider probably influenced your friends and acquaintances not to do business with that person or even his or her entire company. We tend to tell far more people about experiences that made us angry or disappointed than about experiences that left us satisfied or even pleased.

Here's why all this matters. We are *all* involved to a greater or lesser degree in the daily activity of giving or receiving service. In many of the world's greatest commercial centers (such as Hong Kong, London, Los Angeles, San Francisco, New York and Singapore) the lion's share of GDP stems from service sector revenue, not manufacturing.

We depend on good service for the smooth, unruffled running of our personal and professional lives. When service breaks down, one or more aspects of our lives break down. A botched wholesale shipment can mean lost retail sales for a merchant. A rushed, inconsiderate manner by a health provider can discourage a patient from telling his or her full story of recent symptoms—a story necessary for accurate diagnosis and treatment of illness. An inattentive, distracted clerk at a clothing store can flip our inner switch, reminding us "never to go back there again."

We experience the results of service, good or bad, but seldom give much thought to the nature of service itself—what it is, how it can be taught, and how it can be monitored and managed. Service in this way is like the weather. We enjoy it or suffer from it, depending on whether it is sunny or stormy, comfortable or stifling. But we often don't give enough thought to preparing for it or making an effort to control it.

So to the purpose of this book: to spell out the 25 core principles that define service across business and professional sectors, describe how it can be inculcated in the workplace and in our schools and universities, and encouraged and managed by *service leaders* in all walks of life.

Although not written primarily or exclusively for teachers, this book is a "curriculum" of sorts for anyone who wants to understand service more deeply and manage it more effectively in personal and professional life—and that readership includes virtually all of us.

Such a curriculum has long been missing in action. Since the beginnings of the Industrial Revolution, company training programs and business schools have focused on instructing workers how to *make* things.

25 Principles of Service Leadership

But the vast majority of us no longer create or assemble products as our work activity. Instead, we serve others and, in turn, rely on services from others. Our professional success and, to a large extent, our personal satisfaction derives from the quality of the service we provide and receive.

Unfortunately, company training programs and school curricula at all levels have been slow to recognize that *teaching people how to serve* has now become a more pressing and universal need than teaching people how to make things. The Manufacturing Era in most developed countries is passing the torch to the Service Era.

This book contains 25 principles intended as beacons to enlighten and reveal the landscape of service we all experience (or wish to experience) in daily life. A principle without an accompanying response, of course, is like the proverbial "one hand clapping." Therefore, as you consider each of the 25 principles, take a few moments not only to reflect on its meaning and implications in your own life and organization, but also to *make application* of the principle at hand in large and small ways, the sooner the better.

25 Principles of Service Leadership

Specifically, if you supervise others, think of ways in which the principle can improve the service they give to your customers—and the service you give to your employees. If you are a sole practitioner in a profession, use each principle in this book as a lens to help you see yourself and your professional activities through the eyes of your clients.

How do they *feel* in your presence? Do you communicate a *sincere, caring attitude* toward them? Do you make an effort, through concerned and careful listening, to *understand* their needs and problems?

If you are a leader of an organization, use each principle (in addition to the suggestions above) to ask systemic questions: how can the service principle at hand be made part of the culture of the organization—a "must-have," not merely a "nice-to-have," for those you employ? How can you lead your team to perceive the extraordinary benefits of giving excellent service and, on the other hand, the devastating and often irreparable results of delivering inadequate and disappointing service? How can you measure progress among your employees in improving their level of service? How can that progress best be rewarded?

25 Principles of Service Leadership

The plan of this book is straight-forward. Each of the 25 core principles is stated, then briefly explained in concept. In the commentary section, a memorable example or story usually follows, in all cases drawn from real world situations even in those cases where company or individual names have been replaced to protect confidentiality or privacy. Finally, the discussion of each principle concludes with guiding questions intended to lead the reader into meaningful reflection on the principle and an individualized plan to actualize that principle in one's own professional and personal life.

The Sources of the 25 Principles

It is a fair question to ask where these 25 principles come from. No one person created them, although they are gathered here in this form and order for the first time. Each principle has deep roots in the scholarly literature of service leadership, the age-old precepts of worldwide religions and social philosophies, the best practices of successful companies and professionals, and the decades of experience, observation, and reflection of the authors.

The ultimate credential of each principle, however, is its power to produce positive results in the reformation of giving and receiving service in your career, company, and personal relationships. In short, these principles are intended to earn their keep by honing your own expertise and influence as a service leader.

Distinguishing Service from Largesse

Recently, a phalanx of 30 MBA students set themselves the task of collecting, insofar as possible, the great majority of customer service anecdotes (whether from customers, companies, "complaint" sites, and so forth) appearing on the Internet. A fascinating phenomenon began to emerge from the thousands of customer service narratives they collected. Most of these stories were *not* focused on the legitimate fulfillment of the service relationship established between companies and customers.

Instead, they were stories of what we will call "largesse"—tales of companies giving disappointed or disgruntled customers exponentially more than the customer had bargained for. Examples include the shoe and apparel company, Zappos, sending a grandmother six pairs of shoes gratis when the pair she bought didn't fit well; Morton's Steak House sending a fully-prepared steak dinner to greet a businessman who had a tight connection at an airport and had expressed his disappointment at not having time to visit his favorite Morton's restaurant; and Nordstrom's giving an entire rack of expensive clothing away for free when a steady customer complained of less-than-diligent service on the part of her Nordstrom personal shopper.

Is such largesse what we are seeking when we discuss principles of good customer service? *Absolutely not!* Although companies certainly have the right, like kings and queens of old, to give away whatever they wish, *largesse is not the goal or the primary process of delivering exemplary customer service.*

On the one hand, it could be argued that a company makes a customer very happy (and quite surprised) by gifting him or her with products or services far beyond what was promised or expected. But such moments of joy for one or even a few customers is not sustainable over the long term of bona fide customer service relationships. In a word, it is not scalable.

Largesse may make for great company "PR" as the story is told and re-told. However, it differs *in no way* from Roman emperors throwing out coins to paupers or Good King Wenceslas of Christmas legend seeking out a single serf as the beneficiary of a Yuletide banquet.

25 Principles of Service Leadership

Put in another context, if you agree to provide service for a set fee to paint my house, I do not expect you to suddenly announce that you will do the job for free nor that you will continue to paint my house through the years as it passes from owner to owner. The principles of excellence in customer service relationships do *not* require the service provider (as Internet anecdotes tend to suggest) to ignore the contracted terms of service or "give away the farm" without concern for company welfare or profit, all in an effort to amaze one customer with a treasure hoard of unexpected gifts.

That model may fit a lottery, but it certainly does not fit what I mean by excellent customer service.

Although companies often go beyond the call of duty in their efforts to please their customers, the goal is always to fulfill the promised service relationship. As one customer put it well, "I don't expect a company to give me anything for free and, frankly, I would feel a bit embarrassed accepting over-the-top gifts and other free benefits that I never contracted for. I do expect a service provider to be true to their word and, if I experience service problems, to do what they can to resolve those problems quickly and fairly. Sometimes this resolution process may mean that the company spends more on our relationship than they intended. But I'm not a child and I don't expect any service provider to heap extraordinary gifts on me in an effort to somehow impress or surprise me. I'm an adult who respects service providers who deliver what they promise to, in a friendly and flexible way."

Principle 1: The Principle of 15 Minutes of Leadership

The Concept:

The famous artist Andy Warhol coined the phrase "fifteen minutes of fame"—but he was talking about fifteen minutes in a *lifetime*. In the world of service leadership, a person must be prepared to act creatively as a leader (in other words, *be* a leader and decision-maker) for at least fifteen minutes *every hour*.

At Scandinavian Airlines, for example, employees are empowered to make problem-resolving decisions for customers up to a certain limit, as described in *Moment of Truth*, by SAS former CEO Jan Carlzon. These decisions can range from crediting back a charge for a heavy bag, making custom exceptions for in-flight meals, and even "watching the kids" while a customer makes a brief, important phone call from the waiting area.

It would be easy to say "no" to these requests—but Scandinavian Airlines decided it made much better business sense to say "yes" as often as possible. Only the employees who interface with customers can make those on-the-spot, "yes" decisions. Therefore, those were the employees that Scandinavian Airlines freed to make leadership decisions.

Another example involves a dinner occasion. I learned that I would be meeting a small group made up of Indian, Chinese, and Caucasian business people. When the waiter came to table to take our order, he paused to let the Indian client know that the Caesar salad was prepared with bacon (in case the client was a practicing Muslim or Hindu believer, in which case bacon is religiously forbidden).

Could the waiter simply have taken the order for Caesar salad, then let the chips (bacon chips, in this case) fall where they may? Of course. But the result would have been unfortunate for all concerned. The waiter metaphorically used part of his "fifteen minutes" to rise to an act of independent service leadership by trying to resolve a potential problem before it emerged.

Commentary:

As mentioned earlier, the American pop artist Andy Warhol is credited with envisioning a media-drenched day when "everyone will be famous for 15 minutes." I apply this clever wisdom to service leadership in this way: each of us will have the spotlight of leadership focused on us for a relatively brief period before it moves on to another person or group.

How we use that 15 minutes (metaphorically, of course—the actual time may vary from 15 seconds to 15 years or more!) of prominence is crucial in several ways. During our spotlighted moment, we have the opportunity to define ourselves as leaders in the eyes of others—who we are, what we stand for, where we're going. At the same time, we have the chance to influence others by our example—what Kouzes and Posner in The Leadership Challenge (fifth edition, 2015) call "modeling the way." Finally, we have the platform of temporary prominence to enable others to become better partners in the shared activity of service.

Put another way, our 15 minutes of fame as service leaders gives us not only the opportunity to steer the bus but also to show others how to drive—and, beyond that, to welcome their hand on the wheel along with our own.

25 Principles of Service Leadership

Principle 2: The Principle of Self-Leadership

The Concept:

Self-leadership asks us to picture each human being as a composite of two halves: one half of the person's being is inward and reflective—the place where morals, values, and the roots of creativity reside. This part of the individual is rarely seen by the outside world. The other half of a person's being is "delivery-oriented," whether by physical or verbal means. This aspect of our being is definitely seen by the outside world, and our reputation depends to a remarkable degree on what others see.

Self-leadership is the active monitoring and correction by the unseen self of the actions and words of the publically observed self. Leaders who are adept in the art of using intra-personal qualities to control interpersonal actions and communications are judged by others to "mean what they say"—in short, to have integrity and deserve trust.

A story may make this point clear. A mother took her son to see Mahatma Gandhi. She asked the venerable leader to tell her son not to eat a certain Indian sweet because it was bad for his health. The Mahatma told the mother and son to come back in two weeks. They agreed. After the two weeks had passed, the mother with her son returned again to the Mahatma and asked him to tell her son to shun sweets.

Mahatma Gandhi looked steadily at the boy and told him solemnly not to eat sweets because they were bad for his health. After the boy had stepped out of the room, the mother asked the Mahatma why he could not have said these words two weeks earlier. The Mahatma smiled and whispered to her, "Two weeks ago I was eating these same sweets."

The point is this: a leader cannot live an outer life that conflicts with or contradicts his or her inner life. The Mahatma could only speak against the sweets once he, too, had given them up.

Of course, self-leadership has its hazards when the inner self proves immoral or unwise. History is full of examples of malevolent actions that grew directly out of a leader's evil nature and misguided inner thoughts. But interaction with others, if observed carefully and acted on, can have a wonderful purifying effect on the inner self.

25 Principles of Service Leadership

If we observe that we are perpetually disappointing and harming those around us, it is obvious that we need to take stock of our deepest internal values and beliefs that are causing that result. We suggest that people like Bill Gates and Warren Buffett probably experienced a transition along these lines as they realized, over the course of years, that massive amounts of money alone would not bring happiness to themselves or others. They deserve the international praise they receive for turning their fortunes toward solving the world's most pressing problems instead of hoarding wealth for their private pleasures.

Commentary:

At one time or another, all of us have supervised others in their work within organizations and companies, or even clubs and civic efforts. Our supervision takes the form sharing a vision, setting (and usually negotiating) specific goals with those we supervise, encouraging their positive efforts and discouraging negative behavior, monitoring progress, and eventually celebrating and rewarding achievement.

Importantly, these ways in which we manage others can and should be applied to the art of self-leadership. This kind of self-management does not have to conjure up a difficult dualism in which a "little boss inside" calls the shots for the "big body." Instead, it expresses an integrated perspective in which we each think about what we want (goals), why we want it (rationale), how we will go about getting it (strategy and tactics) , and whom will be affected by our actions (ethics and social responsibility).

This period of reflection may be brief indeed—a few thoughtful minutes at the beginning of the day, perhaps, or a brief "check-in" with oneself during break periods or meals during the day. We don't want to be "accidental tourists" on the journey of life, including our professional lives. Through self-leadership, we can apply a variant of the Golden Rule: "Do unto oneself what you would do unto others" in the context of service leadership.

When this approach is applied consistently and in a disciplined way, we sometimes discover that we ourselves can't (or don't want to) measure up to the rigorous standards we set for those we supervise. Self-leadership in this case has taught us the humility of recognizing that achieving goals is not as easy as stating them.

25 Principles of Service Leadership

On the other hand, as we make progress in "getting into shape" within as a self-leader, we not only gain confidence that we can "walk the talk" (that is, show by our actions what we espouse with our voice) but also that the goals we set are achievable, both for ourselves as leaders and for those we lead. Put simply, if you can lead yourself in positive, productive, and healthful ways, that's the best "tell" (in sailing terms) that you can also lead others.

25 Principles of Service Leadership

Principle 3: The Principle of People Leadership

The Concept:

Our first experience of observing and becoming a leader of people occurs most often in the family unit. We observe the leadership behavior of our father and mother (and perhaps grandfather and grandmother), then try those leadership skills on our brothers, sisters, and extended family. Sometimes, of course, we have our first efforts at leadership shoved in our face: "You're not the boss of me!", one of our siblings may shout.

From such experiences we gradually hone our people leadership skills so they become important tools for our success in relating to the world beyond the family—the outside world where we make our livings and provide not only for ourselves but our loved ones as well. Note that the skills I am discussing here have nothing to do with building a product of any kind. These are relational skills, and they matter intensely to our professional and personal success.

25 Principles of Service Leadership

Unfortunately, the current educational system from its earliest grades through graduate school has not devoted enough thought, planning, and delivery strategies to the broad area of people leadership. If the art of relating to others is taught at all, it is taught by a largely ungoverned mentoring system. In British education, for example, those in the Sixth Form teach those in the Fourth Form what kinds of behavior will be tolerated and which will not. In American education, this student-to-student mentoring takes place in large part on sports teams.

Relying on students who themselves are still immature in their people leadership skills to teach other students is wrong-headed. That is why organizations such as the Hong Kong Institute of Service Leadership & Management is working so hard to convince administrators and professors of one central truth: the so-called "soft skills" (those involved in relationships with others) are crucial to a student's eventual success as a worker and as a person.

Nurturing the student's "emotional intelligence" is at least as important (and some would say more important) that the current academic focus on content mastery.

25 Principles of Service Leadership

Examples of excellent people leadership skills are not difficult to find. Hong Kong's immigration officers, though they are immersed in a massive bureaucracy, nevertheless maintain a spirit of friendliness, courtesy and good humor precisely at those locations where humanity needs an emotional helping hand, such as at the extremely busy Hong Kong International Airport. Immigration officers around the world could learn valuable lessons in "emotional intelligence" from these Hong Kong service leaders.

Commentary:

In eighteenth century England, as entire counties were cleared of their inhabitants by the Enclosure Movement and the lure of the industrial jobs in major cities, many English ministers found themselves in an odd dilemma: they had a lifetime sinecure (guaranteed career) as the cleric for a particular church, but it no longer had any parishioners. In hundreds of instances during these decades, English ministers stood up in the pulpit each Sunday and delivered their sermons to entirely empty churches.

They perceived their "job" as writing a sermon and delivering it. Whether or not people heard the sermon was a secondary concern, and one that was often overlooked entirely.

25 Principles of Service Leadership

True service leaders cannot conceive of a business, professional, organizational, or civic context in which their leadership tasks can be fulfilled without connection to and relationship with real people. All service leadership is people leadership. It is no more possible to be a service leader without involvement with people than it is to be a car salesman who claims, "I sold the car but he didn't buy."

The act of selling implies and requires the act of buying. Similarly, the activities of leadership always are influenced by and responsible to the people involved in the service relationship. Service leaders should not be found sermonizing to "empty churches." Instead, their work is tied inextricably to the needs and responses of actual people.

Principle 4: The Principle of the Server

The Concept:

All societies, in spite of their formal policies, have a pecking order of sorts. Usually, those providing a service requiring very little knowledge fall toward the bottom of that social order. Those whose service requires a high degree of knowledge—a brain surgeon, let's say—are ranked toward the top of the social order.

Without justifying the morality or common sense of this pecking order, we can at least recognize that it exists. The question then becomes how to understand our individual roles within the social order, as people who simultaneously provide and receive service.

An example will make this concept clear: when you dial out for food to be delivered to your home, you are providing an economic service to the food provider. When that restaurant responds by delivering what you ordered, you are the recipient of their service. In these countless give-and-take transactions every day, we usually don't attach perceptions of status to the role of the server or the served. Instead, we recognize that they are mutually dependent and therefore are to be mutually valued.

It is a healthy mental exercise (and indeed a "best practice") to play out this idea of mutual dependency to the highest levels of our professional lives as service leaders. Let's say, for example, that you supervise 500 people in a mid-sized corporation. Each of those employees seeks to be of service to you, your goals, and the aspirations of the company as a whole. Without this spirit of employee service, you would inevitably end up with the dilemma of "a chief with no Indians."

But at the same time, you are not simply the recipient of the service of others, like some medieval king or queen. Instead, your work life is comprised of providing service to others, including your employees and customers, in the form of the words you speak or write, the actions you take, and the totality of the life you live. In the famous phrase of James Kouzes and Barry Posner in *The Leadership Challenge*, you "model the way."

Your role as a service leader helps to define what "service" means in your organization. To that extent, you raise the bar for a constructively competitive spirit among all team members. When others see what you do as a leader who serves, they are motivated to give their best as employees who serve. In fact, within their individual work units, they may come to think of themselves as leaders of projects, initiatives, and quality control within their area of influence.

Here's the main point: those who work for you don't abuse their degree of leadership because they don't see you, the organizational leader, abusing your degree of leadership. They recognize that they, like you, are involved in a constant interchange of giving and receiving service.

Commentary:

Imagine for a moment a world devoid of servers, with each man and woman "out for their own" without regard for the welfare of one another. That social model is, of course, impossible, as our very evolution has determined. We are not only homo sapiens—the "knowing human"—but also homo sociologicus—the human aware of and responsive to social connection.

While we might take pride in our rugged individualism, we simultaneously acknowledge that we stand on the shoulders of giants and that our individual strength draws as much from the surrounding human community as from our own wit and courage.

The point here is Rudyard Kipling's in his famous Law of the Jungle: "Now this is the Law of the Jungle -- as old and as true as the sky; And the Wolf that shall keep it may prosper, but the Wolf that shall break it must die. As the creeper that girdles the tree-trunk the Law runneth forward and back --For the strength of the Pack is the Wolf, and the strength of the Wolf is the Pack."

The Principle of the Server suggests that there is nothing weak, compromising, or "subordinate" in serving the needs of others. No doubt in the Pleistocene Age, the adaptation among our ancestors to serve one another's needs (especially in a camp environment or in distributing the bounty of the hunt) was an important civilizing and socially stabilizing force in the onward march of human evolution.

Many world religions and ethical systems, including Confucianism and the Judeo-Christian tradition, have pointed to altruism (especially when it does not lead to self-annihilation) as a noble human quality worthy to be listed among the Thirteen Virtues as well as the Ten Commandments.

25 Principles of Service Leadership

Although few of us literally have prolonged "interior dialogues" with ourselves, such self-reflection for the Server might go as follows: "In following my impulse to serve, I am exercising one of my oldest, most authentic traits as a human being. Serving others does not mean that I am putting myself 'beneath' them or openly myself up to abusive treatment.

"Instead, I am engaging in the activity that originally formed and still forms the 'social glue' binding society together in relative harmony and mutual caring."

Kant (who couldn't help himself as a German systematician!) phrased this concept in a more complicated but nonetheless memorable way in his famous Categorical Imperative: "Behave in such a way that your actions may become Universal Law." (trans.)

The Principle of the Server asserts that service is a higher level, significantly evolved human activity that deserves admiration and emulation from others as well as self-respect and the satisfaction of making a social contribution within the Server.

25 Principles of Service Leadership

Principle 5: The Principle of Competence, Character, and Caring (the Three C's)

The Concept:

Many library shelves can be filled with books purporting to list the core characteristics of a leader. For many scholars, the net result of studying these books is the conclusion that "opinions vary widely." I will attempt to avoid such paralysis by analysis by suggesting that the heart of service leadership lies in three demonstrated (not theoretical) qualities:

- **Competence**
- **Character**
- **Caring**

When these qualities are present, an individual's role and ongoing status as a service leader is virtually assured. In many cases, the individual is credited with "charisma," which is nothing more or less than personal magnetism that inspires trust, hope, and confidence in others.

Competence in one's areas of responsibility gets the individual to the first rung on the ladder to true service leadership success. All the best intentions in the world are useless if the individual lacks the knowledge and skill sets to perform well on the job. An example of good intentions without competence can be found in the way many nations appoint their ambassadors. In the United States, for example, at least half of all ambassador appointments to foreign countries are based on political patronage—and specifically the amount of money an individual has raised for the national leader's campaign chest. When the U.S. President informs an individual that they have been chosen to be an ambassador to a foreign post, the individual is no doubt very pleased and filled with good intentions for the new job.

But does that individual's ability to raise money for political campaigns a fair index of their competence to serve as an ambassador? Sadly, no. Too many politically appointed ambassadors end up as international vacationers, without a cogent vision of what they could be doing as an ambassador or how to go about doing it.

Character refers to an individual internalized set of values—the inner integrity that allows the individual to withstand criticism from those who disagree with him or her and the authenticity to "stand for something" instead being blown haphazardly by the winds of influence and opinion.

25 Principles of Service Leadership

It is fair to say that almost none of us has taken a school course focusing on character. Secondary and tertiary schools in particular have seemed to adopt a "hands-off" policy when it comes to the discussion of character, much less recommendations for its formation. The story goes that, after the end of World War II, Harvard University found its lecture halls filled with returning soldiers taking classes with the financial help of the G.I. Bill. Harvard's diverse faculty met to discuss the question of teaching values, and especially *which* values to teach.

Sides quickly formed, accompanied by rampant suspicion. Conservative faculty worried that liberal professors would steep their students in the principles of communism. Liberal faculty, at the same time, were apprehensive that conservative professors would teach personal and social values closely aligned to fundamentalist religious tenets.

The result of this epic faculty squabble was that no action was taken one way or the other in the matter of teaching values (and personal character growing out of one's values). Princeton, Berkeley, Yale and other leading educational institutions followed Harvard's lead. Teaching values quickly became synonymous with proselytizing for one's own subjective opinions as a professor.

25 Principles of Service Leadership

While we would all admit that cramming one set of values down an individual's throat is morally and educationally wrong, we would also admit, I believe, that ignoring a topic as important as that of the formation of character is equally fool-hearty. Secondary and tertiary institutions are charged worldwide with contributing positively to the formation of the mature individual. That formation cannot take place if "values" and "character" are forbidden words in the classroom.

Caring hardly requires explanation, since it is an emotional "must have" for each of us in our development from infant to adulthood and through old age. Caring is equally important for companies who want to develop trust relationships with their clients—an emotional, unselfish bond that communicates respect, concern, and a willingness to act in the client's interest. "I continue to do business with Company X because the people there really care" is perhaps the highest compliment that can be given in the world of business and organizational life.

Commentary:

Gustav Flaubert has been loosely translated as asserting that "the devil is in the details." It's one thing to aspire to "service." It's quite another to put

46

meat on those bones and know, for oneself and in guiding others, what constitutes the heart and soul of excellent service.

Competence suggests that good intentions for service are not enough. An ignorant physician who means to serve the patient well by taking out an inflamed appendix by crude and dangerous methods has mis-served his profession, the patient, and his own reputation. Viewed as a value proposition, therefore, a crucial element of the service relationship between the server and the served is the presence of "something worthwhile."

The linguistic root of the 'competence' from Latin through Old French is 'com,' meaning 'together,' and 'pet-ere,' meaning 'to aim.' Therefore, the word 'competence' came to mean not aiming at one's own individual goals, but instead being able to hit the target which together we define as desirable or worthwhile. Someone competent in service is not merely possessed of an individual aptitude or ability; he or she knows the general standard by which others judge competence, and is willing to be measured by that standard.

Put into the terms of a few professions, a lawyer is not competent because he or she can recite a given snippet of legal precedent; rather, his or her competence is demonstrated by making that legal knowledge meaningful in the social context of a court of law or other proceeding. A civic leader is not proven competent by the ability to draw an organizational chart, but instead to organize the individuals on that chart into a productive work team. Competence is socially determined and socially judged.

The word 'character' can similarly be enlightened by its word origin, in this case stemming from the Greek word *charakter*, meaning "an engraved mark." The wisdom, followed at DHL for decades and at many other global corporations, is to "hire for character, train for skills." Referring to the old Greek sense of the word, this means that certain traits are "engraved" within an individual long before he or she applies for work with the company.

Among these traits are a strong disposition toward honesty, a willingness to work with others, a patient and receptive attitude in receiving advice and criticism, and a firm personal grounding in appropriate workplace behaviors, including the avoidance of sexual harassment, verbal abuse, and other undesirable work behaviors.

25 Principles of Service Leadership

If an individual comes to the hiring process deeply flawed in these areas, it is unlikely that any company training program or mentoring effort will be successful, let's say, in turning a workplace lecher into a trustworthy colleague able to relate professionally to both men and women in the office.

Part of the art of the hiring interview, therefore, is to listen and probe for indications of character flaws. Why did the applicant leave his or her last job? How does a male applicant feel about having a female boss, or vice versa? What would an applicant consider a serious theft (in time, money, or property) from the company versus a trivial offense that could be overlooked? What kind of people rub the applicant the wrong way? How does the applicant like to be managed?

These kinds of questions can open windows to the applicant's character. Handled skillfully by a trained interviewer, such questions can get interviews to reveal much more about themselves than they intended—information that can invaluable to the hiring employer who seeks new hires who bring solid, reliable character traits to their first day on the job.

'Caring' comes from the Old English 'caru,' with the interesting and unexpected meaning of "sorrow, anxiety, grief." That's a whole different perspective on what it means to serve with "care." We usually understand the word 'care' in its less intensive meanings, along the lines of "concern, consideration, or special attention."

But we should take seriously the old and important roots of the word 'care': the Anglo-Saxons meant by that word that you felt deep and often painful emotions if things weren't going right in a particular relationship or situation.

Imagine how different the world of service would be if that ancient meaning of "care" was restored to our sensibility. Can you picture a postal employee feeling sincere grief or anxiety when a registered letter addressed to you can't be found in the post office? Those kinds of emotions would convince even the most skeptical customer of the post office that its employees really care.

Or imagine a phone call from your financial advisor; she says she has been upset for hours over the implications of new tax legislation as it applies to you, and wants to talk to you right away about the best course of action. Now that's an accountant to hang onto!

25 Principles of Service Leadership

Caring, in short, has to go beyond the casual meaning of 'concern' to significant emotions of grief, anxiety, and sadness as the server tries to understand how to resolve the problem. We still use the word 'care' in its older context when, in love relationships, we say 'I care deeply for you.' That phrase does not mean that we occasionally think about the other person or that they are 'on our list' of people to 'friend' on Facebook.

In strong personal relationships, to 'care' means to open oneself to empathy ("feeling with," not "feeling for") that includes the probably of worrying about the person, feeling grief over their misfortunes, and doing what you can to restore their happiness.

Service in the business and professional world, of course, is not a love relationship. But true service can't be flippant; it either draws upon our sincere emotions of a degree of anxiety and/or sorrow over the dilemma of the person we are trying to serve, or it is not worthy of the name. Unselfishness is the key in dealing constructively with service issues of all kinds.

The corporate motto of Johnson & Johnson worldwide is "Because We Care." As a medical company serving at times the most desperate of human physical and emotional needs, Johnson &

25 Principles of Service Leadership

Johnson means these words in their most profound sense: the company is deeply aware of physical and emotional suffering in the world and works hard to cure or alleviate it, in close communication and partnership with its clients.

Principle 6: The Principle of Co-created Service Leadership

The Concept:

No service leader can or should make a unilateral decision on the type, timing, nature, or extent of service for a client. In simple examples, a hairdresser does not decide how to cut or style a customer's hair without frequent and detailed input from the person in the chair. An architect pays elaborate attention to the client's needs and wishes before beginning to draw up blueprints.

Service is co-created between the service provider and the service receiver. Put another way, service is not a pre-packaged commodity delivered on a "take it or leave it" basis. Of course, we are discussing here those services intended to build an on-going relationship with the customer. It is true that some companies have only a pre-determined "service package" to offer, no matter what the individual needs of the customer. Unfortunately, too many "services" offered in the form of university classes are pre-packaged, without regard for the actual learning styles or preferences of the student "customers."

25 Principles of Service Leadership

A world-famous model of co-created service has been championed for many years by Nordstrom's, the giant clothing department store. Nordstrom provides a "personal shopper" who gets to know the customer's tastes, budget, and wish list. The sales transaction that eventually takes place has been co-created through caring conversation between the Nordstrom employee (the service provider in this case) and the customer (the service receiver).

The importance of the idea of co-creation is precisely this: a service leader must spend at least as much time and effort in listening (and then responding) to the needs and wishes of the customer as on the design and delivery of the intended service. In a literal sense, it is not possible to design and deliver what the customer really wants apart from the process of co-creation.

Commentary:

In 1794, the mystic English poet William Blake wrote these lines in The Human Abstract: "Pity would be no more / If we did not make someone Poor." Service, particularly when it is viewed as largesse provided from a wealthy, empowered person or group to an impoverished, disempowered person or group, can have the look and feel of condescension.

In such cases, service is perceived as "one way": the needy person is the passive recipient while the serving person is the active giver. (In this regard, recall the opening remarks in this book on the false role of "largesse" as a company substitute for legitimate, system-wide customer service.)

What often emerges out of these types of relationships (termed "I/Thou" relationships by the theologian and philosopher Martin Buber) is increasing dominance on the part of the giver ("I'll give what I want") and increasing helplessness on the part of the recipient ("I'll take anything I can get").

Hence Blake's judgment that a relationship based on pity ends up making all parties the poorer for the experience.

Service is a two-way proposition, "co-created" in the sense that both the server and the person served play active roles in the relationship. Both set boundaries and expectations that help the service relationship succeed.

Take, for example, the services of a florist at the wedding. The wedding planner or family can't sit back passively and expect the florist to "read their minds" as to what flowers are required, how they will be arranged, and when they will be delivered. Instead, these items are carefully specified by the party being served, down to the exact time when the flower arrangements must be completed in the place of worship or wedding reception area.

In the process of indicating their requirements, the party being served may also indicate some areas of flexibility, either in time or in types of flowers based on market availability. The serving party, in the same way, also establishes boundaries and expectations. A price for services, for example, is usually agreed upon in advance. The number and general description of bouquets and other flower arrangements is placed in a contract.

When the service of providing the wedding flowers is ultimately successful, to the delight of the bride and groom as well as to the satisfaction of the florist, clearly the service involved has been "co-created"— the input and communication of both parties were crucial throughout the process for the service to be successful.

It is not uncommon for service providers to discover that the party they intend to serve is not familiar with the general idea of "co-created service." The party to be served may say, in effect, "I turned that over to you and now it's your responsibility."

That kind of abdication of the responsibility of co-creation can spell disaster in many service relationships. Imagine a surgeon, for example, being told by a patient, "I want you to restore me to health through your services, but don't expect anything from me along the line." No surgeon would accept such a person as a patient, precisely because the outcome of the service would likely be unsuccessful indeed.

Medical professionals quickly learn to make their patients "partners in the enterprise of health" instead of patients waiting for someone else to cure them. Proper diet, exercise, stress reduction, consistent use of prescribed medications, and so forth can all be ways in which a patient "co-creates" the service he or she desires from a physician.

The same general idea applies to service across most business and professional sectors. Recipients of service wisely recognize that when they do their part (as defined by or negotiated with the service provider), the service relationship has a much better chance of success.

The reverse situation, of course, is also common. The server may "play dumb," waiting for the party to be served to describe all aspects of the service relationship. Sometimes this posturing on the part of the server is an effort to avoid eventual blame—"If this doesn't turn out well, don't blame me. I just did what you told me to."

Anyone seeking service needs to draw upon the server's competence, as described earlier, as part of the necessary two-way input into any service understanding or agreement. In common parlance, this kind of communication challenges both parties to "live up to their ends of the bargain" and, thus, co-create the service relationship they both desire.

Principle 7: The Principle of Knowing Who You Are

The Concept:

In both Eastern and Western philosophic and religious traditions, we are strongly advised to observe not only a person's words but especially their behavior (Confucius) to know who they are—or, applied personally, to "know thyself" (Socrates). A service leader makes it a habit to reflect on his or her actions, attitudes, relationships with others, written and spoken words, and other personal attributes. The goal of this self-examination is not to rate oneself as superior or inferior in relation to others, but instead to locate areas for self-improvement in a continuous quest to deserve the confidence of others around you.

We should pay attention not only to our best selves in show-case situations, but also to impulsive words and actions when we know we are not "on stage," so to speak. These moments, as Confucius counseled, include times when we are angry, playing mah-jong or another game with friends, or simply going out for a drink with others. If we discover ourselves to be ethically weak or interpersonally offensive at such times, we can hardly claim to "have our act together" when called upon to take up the challenges of service leadership.

This is not to say that we should demand perfection of ourselves in every waking moment. But we should be observant of "who we really are" in both our private and public moments—and then use those observations to come ever closer to the person and leader we aspire to be.

Commentary:

We look upon service as a "present tense" experience. It would be unusual, for example, to check in to a fine hotel, receive poor service, and think to oneself, "No problem. They gave me good service when I stayed here last year." Service, for better or worse, is one of those "what have you done for me lately" experiences. It happens in the present moment or doesn't happen at all.

This "present tense" concept means that both the server and the served bring their in-the-moment, present selves to the service transaction. Put another, both parties need to know who they are, not just who they were or who they want to be in the future.

25 Principles of Service Leadership

Therefore, let's address that crucial question: Who are you? Your resume may contain hints and "trend lines" about who you are, but that document is essentially about your past, not your present. Similarly, your aspirations and dreams are an important component of your personality, but they depict a "future you," not the in-the-moment person.

A sincere, adaptive service transaction demands that you know who you are during the period of that connection. Are you distracted by other priorities? Are you letting emotions from a recent experience of some kind wash over into this service moment? Are you making assumptions about the person you are serving that may not be accurate? Are you quieting your own mind so that you can truly listen to what the other person is telling you (by verbal as well as non-verbal communication)?

Many spiritual and philosophic traditions offer counsel for addressing the question "who am I?" and then using the answers we find to help ourselves and others. Buddhism, for example, emphasizes the importance of meditation and prospect of enlightenment as a way of finding ourselves wholly in the moment and not looking in the rearview mirror toward our past or mentally jumping ahead to worry about our future.

25 Principles of Service Leadership

Such meditation need not be prolonged or even noticeable. Self-awareness (the answer to the question "who am I" at this moment) can be aided by even the briefest deep breath of reflection—a personal "break" in which we pack away the past for the time being and push out future concerns, freeing ourselves for that precious experience of being open to the full range of sensations, information, and insights that can flood in from the present.

Why is self-awareness so important to a service relationship? Probably on many occasions, we have all experienced poor service from a person who "isn't there," who obviously isn't listening to what we are saying, and who simply wants to move us along so that he can get back to what he was doing.

We feel like saying to such a distracted person, "Look, I'm right here face to face with you. Focus, for heaven's sake! I'm willing to give you my full attention and I want yours." Successful service relationships can't blossom from individuals who are scattering the seeds of their attention and caring elsewhere at the moment. Both the server and the served, as co-creators of the service relationship, need to bring themselves fully to the moment of the service transaction.

25 Principles of Service Leadership

Only by knowing yourself can you bring yourself, in an open, receptive way, to the service relationship.

25 Principles of Service Leadership

Principle 8: The Principle of Personal Ethics

The Concept:

It remains a complex question where our individual ethical standards come from. Some would argue that our parents' ethical code inevitably becomes our own. Others would point to the influence of religion, philosophy, and even friendships in determining our personal ethics.

Without attempting to unravel the genesis of individual ethics, we can nevertheless observe their crucial role for service leaders of all kinds and in all professional sectors. Doing what's right, although often difficult in times of organizational crisis or cutbacks, ultimately defines the leader who can be trusted.

A case in point involves a government leader caught up in a "what-did-you-know-and-when-did-you-know-it" scandal. These career-threatening moments seem to occur in virtually every country on a regular basis. Too often, the accused leader decides to throw organizational subordinates "under the bus" by claiming the problem at hand was their fault, not the leader's.

25 Principles of Service Leadership

Because subordinates have less access to media channels and therefore little opportunity to rebut the leader's charges, they "fall on their swords" by accepting job termination and a distinct black mark against their future career. It is the rare leader indeed who can summon the personal ethical strength to tell the truth, even if that truth reveals his or her own mistakes. Subordinates in an organization trust a leader who does not shrink from telling it like it is instead of telling it like it isn't.

They are willing to follow an ethical leader down the barrel of a cannon. Just the opposite is true once a leader shows his or her true colors through lying and other forms of deception. Subordinates may not confront the leader directly regarding an ethical breach, but they will surely lose their sense of loyalty to him or her. This defection results in absenteeism, lower quality work, and high turnover.

One way for a service leader to clarify and perpetuate important ethical values is to publicize and live by an organizational Code of Ethics. This document, sometimes called a "values" statement, lists the moral standards to which the organization, including all its employees, commits itself. A leader refers to this core list of values often in public and private statements, including media appearances.

25 Principles of Service Leadership

Ethics, once known widely to the public, can be a powerful marketing advantage for a company. Recent events involving Google's and Facebook's use of customer profiles raised moral questions for the public, and these companies have spent many millions of dollars in attempting to enforce an internal code of ethics while at the same time reassuring the public that their data privacy will not be abused.

Commentary:

Doing the right thing as a service leader presumes that you know what the right thing is. Although moral knowledge can be encouraged by company codes of ethics and on-the-job mentoring, your core commitment to a set of personal ethics is primarily something you bring to the job as an attribute of your character. The ultimate source of our moral standards is complex indeed, involving both "nature" and "nurture."

Some of our convictions about right and wrong appear to be hard-wired in our nature as human beings. Others have been taught to us by parents, friends, teachers, religious influences, and the culture(s) in which we grew up and continue to grow.

25 Principles of Service Leadership

Personal ethics are always evolving and adapting as we face new situations in life, make decisions about those situations, and experience the consequences of our decisions. But such daily ethical development notwithstanding, by early adulthood our personal code of ethics must be firmly established within our character if we are to have lasting professional and personal success.

Those suffering from stunted development of ethics too often find themselves caught up in a cascading series of lies, each attempting to "cover" for some earlier untruth or misdeed.

Service leadership apart from a well-developed personal code of ethics is impossible precisely because no one trusts unethical people. Even if the unethical person has not cheated us, simply the knowledge that he acts unethically toward others makes us wary of the relationship and usually sends us in search of a morally sound person with whom to do business and establish an on-going relationship.

What is true of individuals is no less true of companies. Newspaper, magazine, and Internet headlines in every country regularly report the moral breaches of companies who have purposely mis-manufactured or mis-labeled products to increase profit; hidden the abysmal work conditions of their employees from public view; bribed their way to lucrative contracts; and turned a blind eye toward practices of gender, ethnic, and age discrimination in their hiring and firing practices.

In spite of the noble ethical claims in a company's mission statement or code of professional conduct, the words of Socrates still apply: "Know the wise man [or company] by the way he lives." The sum total of a person's or company's ethical standards is measured in actions more than words.

25 Principles of Service Leadership

Principle 9: The Principle of Whom You Hire

The Concept:

Deciding whom to hire in a growing company is not dissimilar to a young couple's decision to have one or more children. You know that the decision will affect your "company" (in business or in family life). You hope, of course, the influence of the new member will be positive. But can you plan in your hiring process to virtually assure that you're hiring well?

Yes and no. A careful review of the resume, references, interview results, and any testing you administer can help you compare candidates. In a manufacturing environment, you are looking for the superior candidate who demonstrates that he or she can *do things right*—that is, maintain a high standard for fulfilling the tasks required in a manufacturing job. These tasks can include monitoring quality control, performing assembly line duties efficiently, handling budgets well, and all the other responsibilities involved in turning raw materials into saleable products.

But in a service environment, you are seeking the outstanding candidate who can *do the right thing*. This distinction may seem to be mere semantics at first, but it proves absolutely crucial to the proper growth and development of any service organization. Hiring the person who can do the right thing means evaluating character and trustworthiness, not just task competence. Often one or more in-office interviews proves insufficient to measure an individual candidate's ability to do the right thing.

For this reason, many service organizations hire for a probationary period, during which high-performing veterans in the company get to know the new individual and assess his or her consistent ability to keep promises, act fairly, and relate professionally (without "blow-ups" or their opposite, inappropriate fraternization), and communicate the desired image of the company to co-workers and customers.

These are the winning candidates who last in service careers and prove loyal to their organizations and supervisors. They are also the hires who contribute creative ideas for problem-solving on the job, since their motivation to do well comes "from the heart," not just from the wallet. They are invested in the ongoing welfare of the company. That commitment shows in everything they do and in every relationship they form.

25 Principles of Service Leadership

Commentary:

It is unfortunate that in many companies the top leaders and their immediate executive team find themselves too busy to become involved in the selection process, except for top echelon hiring. The growth tip of any organization lies in the new employees brought aboard. The process of finding just the right people for such growth should never be "delegated down" to a perfunctory, back-office operation.

Executive leaders stand at the top of a pyramid whose strength depends on the competence, character, and caring of every employee from the base on up through each level of company hierarchy.

Finding that right person for the right job should never be based solely on a consideration of technical abilities. "Hire for character, train for skills" has long been the selection mantra of many successful, progressive companies, including DHL. It is more and more the case that companies have their own proprietary software systems, marketing and sales strategies, and service procedures that are ahead of the curve of what students learn in college or workers bring from previous employment.

25 Principles of Service Leadership

These companies are prepared, therefore, to provide thorough orientation for new hires in what can generally be termed the "technical" aspects of their jobs. What companies can't easily provide—and often cannot provide even with great effort—is sound character on the part of a new hire. Is the person honest? Does the person have concern and caring for the wellbeing and success of other employees in the company and also its customers and other stakeholders? Will the person admit to mistakes and use them as opportunities for learning? Does the person bring a spirit of initiative and enthusiasm to the workplace?

In terms of building a strong, nimble workforce, these broad issues of character far surpass in importance any narrow matters of a particular skill—matters which can often be taught on the job in a day or less.

Companies and organizations of all descriptions should therefore design their hiring processes to reveal character traits and tendencies. Honesty and integrity tests (widely available commercially) can be helpful in this regard. But there is still no substitute for indepth personal conversation and probing to gain insight into an applicant's strengths and flaws of character.

25 Principles of Service Leadership

Consequently, thorough training of interviewers becomes the vital link between what the company seeks in its employees and what it in fact receives through its hiring processes. Interviewers have to know what questions to ask, when and how to probe for feelings and additional information, what simulations or situations to pose to candidates, and what ultimate scheme of evaluation and decision-making to use in order to hire for character.

25 Principles of Service Leadership

Principle 10: The Principle of Authoritarian and Distributed Leadership

The Concept:

Authoritarian leadership—that is, top-down, "command-and-control" authority over people and operations—has gotten a bad rap in our day. It is vaguely associated with overly restrictive parents who never give their children a chance to make their own decisions and judgments. In fact, authoritarian leadership is alive, well, and *needed* in any organization where strict adherence to rules and regulations is paramount to product quality, public safety, and the image and reputation of the company.

Imagine, for example, a pharmaceutical company that had no top-down authority guiding and enforcing the formulation of prescriptions. Just such companies have emerged, briefly, in some countries where "drugs" turned out to be little more than sugar and chalk. As might be expected, those fake enterprises soon found themselves despised by customers and imprisoned by their governments.

25 Principles of Service Leadership

Without discounting the value, therefore, of authoritarian leadership in the right place and for the right reasons, we can consider the power of another leadership style—distributed leadership. This phrase does not mean that every individual in the company gets to invent policies and procedures on a day-to-day basis. Instead, distributed leadership suggests that an organization has been structured so that *appropriate* leadership decisions are pushed down to their lowest practical level.

At DHL, for example, this form of leadership meant empowering couriers to make on-the-spot decisions to advise customers on their best shipping options, organize their courier routes for maximum efficiency, and give constructive feedback to their managers on how to improve the company's services. Notice that they did not make authoritarian decision, such as promotions, ordering of new delivery vans, or creation of tracking software for DHL packages (although their opinions on these matters were considered by top management).

Authoritarian leadership requires little trust, once the company has assured itself that it has the right top managers in place. The nature of business from that point on is making sure that top-down directives are followed accurately the workforce. But in a distributed leadership model, a high degree of trust is required at all levels with the organization. Like soldiers on a battlefield, each member of the organization must trust the motives, judgment and actions of their fellow workers—those who "have their backs" and on whom they depend.

Workers in a distributed leadership environment are guided not so much by the literal "contract" they may have signed at their time of hiring, but rather by the unspoken but very real "covenant" they maintain among themselves, co-workers, and the company. A "covenant" relationship implies that workers act in the intended *spirit* of their employment relationship, not merely according to legalistic agreements.

Lynne G. Zucker has helped us all understand the nature of trust within organizations by defining its three dominant varieties:

- Process-oriented trust grows out of the need for each individual or work unit within a company structure to have confidence in the portion of the service or product as it comes to them. At the global giant supply chain company, Li & Fung, the *process* of fulfilling a customer's wishes involves trust by each person or group within the supply chain that others before them in the organization have done their jobs well. Companies that rely on the power of process-oriented trust invest heavily in training, monitoring, morale-building, and teamwork to ensure that the entire enterprise operates like a well-oiled machine. The rather astounding variety and complexity of fulfillment services achieved by amazon.com are a good example of process-oriented trust at every level of the organization.

- Character-oriented trust focuses on the attributes and deep intentions of the individuals within the organization as the basis of mutual confidence. Nordstrom's, for example, attains its high level of customer service because it hires with extreme care, seeking out those sales candidates who can consistently deliver genuine, caring, and creative service to the company's demanding clientele. Most election-based political systems are similarly based on character-oriented trust, in which the public scrutinizes a political candidate's private and personal life for strong evidence of integrity and high moral standards. An instance of tax evasion, business cheating, sexual misconduct, or other breach of character-oriented trust can quickly destroy the future of a would-be political leader.
- Institution-based trust stems from the orderly structure of rules, regulations, policies, and procedures established and rigorously enforced by an organization. Some car-manufacturing companies, at least for periods of their existence, have risen to this type and level of trust in the public mind. There was a time, in the face of product recalls and

frequent on-the-road breakdowns of U.S.-made autos, that Toyota and Honda (and, more recently, Hyundai) gained the reputation of producing "trustable" automobiles that could go for well over 100,000 miles without need for major repairs. This kind of trust grew not from the public's trust in the employees of those companies (*character*-oriented trust) or in any special difference in the *process* used on the assembly-line, but instead from the public belief that these companies as *institutions* staked their reputations on the quality and durability of their products. In fact, when Toyota moved part of its manufacturing base to the U.S., American managers and workers had to adjust, often with difficulty, to "doing things the Toyota way."

In short, trust underlies whatever leadership style or structure a company puts in place. It is impossible to say in advance of knowing a company's specific circumstances whether authoritarian or distributed leadership will prove to be more effective in achieving that organization's goals. Often a combination of the two styles—authoritarian leadership for rules that must be adhered to, distributed leadership for creative input and on-the-ground service efficiencies—are found in the most successful organizations.

25 Principles of Service Leadership

Commentary:

In egalitarian societies, the mistake is often made to judge "authoritarian" leadership as uniformly bad and "distributed" leadership (with its implied populist preference) as uniformly good. Every experienced professional knows the naivete of such either/or thinking. Especially in times of crisis and fast-moving change, it may be essential for one voice to speak for the company—that of the authoritarian leader.

At other times—let's say, in a period of shifting markets where many options are in play—the same company may depend on leadership decision-making distributed throughout the various divisions and functions of the organization.

Authoritarian leadership has several advantages. First, decisions can be swiftly and communicated clearly (from a single message source) to everyone in the organization. Second, the persona or charismatic nature of the authoritarian leader can inspire the organization with a shared vision and keep work on track and in line with that vision.

Finally, in an era of governmental oversight and regulation, a strong, well-spoken authoritarian leader can serve as the "point of the spear" for the organization, protecting it from its enemies and, through his or her connections, nurturing its alliances with helpful friends.

The downsides of authoritarian leadership are probably more familiar. A leader who insists it's "my way or the highway" tends to surround himself or herself with "yes" lieutenants who tell the leader only what he or she wants to hear. Moreover, a leader who takes on all decision-making robs others in the organization of the chance to develop their own creativity and initiative.

Workers adopt the attitude, "Why bother giving my opinion? The boss is going to make all the decisions anyway." Over time, a workforce emerges that "parks its brains at the curb" when entering the workplace. Last, an authoritarian leader who is thoroughly disliked by the workforce may bring out the worst in employees—poor work habits, frequent absences, high turnover, increased litigation, and even incidents of workplace sabotage and violence. "Acting out" in such ways by employees who consider themselves disrespected and abused is comparable in many ways to the actions of children in a home dominated by a hated parent.

25 Principles of Service Leadership

Distributed leadership also has its pluses and minuses. On the "up" side, it offers leadership opportunities to more people within the organization and thus makes better use of employee talent. As employees find themselves empowered to exercise their intelligence and make good decisions, they become more committed to their job, their coworkers, and the company itself. Morale rises and expensive turnover decreases.

Perhaps most important, decision-making is pushed to the level where it can be most effective. A flight attendant, for example, who is empowered to resolve a $100 customer problem on the spot is a much more efficient decision-maker than a Vice President of Customer Relations who may hear (or not hear) about the incident weeks later.

In this perspective, distributed leadership can be viewed as a spread-out fishnet of sorts. At appropriate times, any portion of the fishnet can be raised to the status of on-the-spot leadership. When the situation at hand is resolved, that portion of the fishnet settles back into its previous position while elsewhere another point of the fishnet rises to the call of leadership.

25 Principles of Service Leadership

Significantly, in distributed leadership environments the top leader of the company does not give away his or her power or authority. Instead, the top leader "deputizes" others in the organization as a way of extending executive authority to levels where it can do the most good at the best time.

For all its merits and popular reputation, distributed leadership is not the answer to all work challenges. In the case of product failure or tampering, for example, the prospect of having several distributed voices of leadership each giving their own explanations and versions of the incident will probably spell media disaster for the company.

Similarly, organizations in which employees are treated quite differently in terms of workload, compensation, and work environment depending on the decisions of their distributed leader may end up in paralyzing workforce bickering and plummeting morale. Distributed leadership also poses the frequent problem of monitoring and control. When should an employee take it upon himself or herself to rise to a position of local leadership?

Just as important, how will that employee know when his or her "15 minutes of leadership" have expired and it is time to rejoin the troops at work? In the same way that "a little knowledge is a dangerous thing," so some companies intent on promoting distributed leadership have discovered that "a little leadership is a dangerous thing."

This observation does not mean that a company should give up its efforts to encourage distributed leadership; rather, it suggests that the key to successful distributed leadership depends on clear policies, skillful mentoring, and flexible but not infinitely elastic job descriptions.

Principle 11: The Principle of Trust, Fairness, Respect, and Care

The Concept:

In a service organization, no large or small print in a contract specifies that the service provider must extend to the customer such nontangible, relational qualities as respect, courtesy, fairness and the trust that results from these qualities. But lacking these qualities, even the most technically "correct" demonstration of service can prove empty and sterile to both the customer and to the service provider.

In many countries, the post office is a prime example of a service rendered without any effort at conveying caring, respect, or courtesy. "I felt like I was being served by a robot," one customer of a U.S. post office complained. And the person providing the service probably didn't feel good about the experience, either. It is discouraging to one's self-image as a professional to know that your customer is feeling disrespected, ignored, or otherwise ill-treated.

The phenomenon of "going postal" (that is, bringing violence into the workplace by employees) testifies to the importance of basic human courtesy in relationships. Lacking them, we too often revert to our worst instincts.

Probably it is beyond the scope of most company training programs to bring about deep changes in a person's commitment to fairness, respect, caring, and other positive human virtues. Certainly one or more training lectures on these "must-have" qualities do not significantly change the behavior of new or experienced employees.

The burden therefore falls upon company hiring practices to select individuals who, by their upbringing, innate character, and previous work experiences, have already learned one of the most important lessons in providing service: how you treat the customer is at least as important as all the other aspects of the transaction combined. A well-treated customer develops trust in the service provider, and keeps coming back for more business even at those times when a modest price premium may arise due to competition or changing market conditions.

On the global stage, a fine example of consistency and high standards in customer treatment is the kind of service provided by the supply chain giant, Li & Fung International. Although the company is legendary for getting a huge array of products to customers on or before the specified delivery date, the firm is equally famous for showing sincere concern, caring, and patience in all their communications and other interactions with their clients.

This approach to customer service includes simple acts such as thanking customers for their business to more complex activities, such as "pulling out all the stops" to resolve unexpected delays that could affect a customer's confidence and trust in the company.

Commentary:

In most famous restaurants, the "hidden ingredients"—those you wouldn't know to add to a similar dish made at home—are the ones that make the chef's meal memorable. In the same way, the service relationship depends on key ingredients that are too often overlooked or underestimated: trust, fairness, respect, and care.

Take, for example, the simple service of walking into a bank to make a deposit. Underlying any thought you may have about the teller's competence or other "surface" items of service are basic assumptions you are making about key ingredients that makes this service recipe work.

First, you trust the bank to hold our money safely and responsibly. (Notice that the bank probably encourages this assumption on your part by the way its employees dress, the neatness of its facility, and in some banks the prominent visibility of a large vault— as much for customer perception as for real safety in this age of electronic funds storage and transfer).

Second, you assume that the bank will be fair to you in all respects. It will not withhold your access to your funds unreasonably or against policies. It will serve you according to place in the customer queue rather than unfairly letting others cut in ahead of you.

Third, you expect a baseline of respect no matter if your deposit is large or small. The bank expresses this respect by insisting that its employees speak to you with courtesy, listen to your concerns, and make every effort to resolve any problems you experience with your account.

Finally, you enter the bank with the expectation that every member of its organization cares about you as a customer and will demonstrate that caring by a) making you aware of any bank information that may affect your finances positively or negatively—for example, a special bank promotion or a new charge being applied to your account; b) taking any problem you experience "up the ladder" as necessary in a timely way to resolve it; and c) showing by the words chosen, facial expressions, and tone of voice that your business with the bank is important and worthy of sincere concern.

Trust, fairness, respect and caring are the "hidden ingredients" that distinguish a successful service experience from an unsuccessful one.

An auto mechanic regularly serviced the expensive car of a well-known heart surgeon. "Doc," the mechanic complained on one service visit, "I don't think it's fair that you earn so much more than I do."

"How so?" the surgeon inquired.

"Well, I replace the spark plug. Take off the head to adjust the valves. Replace the belts. Then I put it all back together again. Basically we do the same thing, but you get paid ten times what I do."

25 Principles of Service Leadership

The doctor smiled. "Try it when it's running."

Principle 12: The Principle of POS (Personal Operating System)

The Concept:

The idea of a POS (Personal Operating System) is an analogy to the DOS (Disk Operating System) of a computer. The DOS operating code lies at such a "deep" level within the programming of a computer that it cannot be easily altered except by computer specialists. From the user's point of view, the DOS system makes the running of programs problem-free.

Like DOS, the POS is involves a "code" of sorts, but not one written in the language of computer programming. POS code is a deep set of rules and behaviors that a person follows by nature, almost without giving them conscious thought. For example, a clerk dealing with a customer's return of an unwanted item demonstrates his or her POS by friendly communication and an expressed desire to resolve the problem to the customer's satisfaction, insofar as possible within company rules.

Even in cases where the customer cannot attain his goal of returning an item (perhaps because it has been extensively worn, and so forth) , that customer should nevertheless feel that the clerk had his interests at heart and was doing all he could to make things right. In short, the customer should feel that the service provider's POS was characterized by honesty, understanding, and caring.

Perhaps we have all had the frustrating experience of dealing with computer problems stemming from a corrupted DOS. Standard commands don't work, programs fail, and the computer itself "freezes up" in the midst of our working session. Often the culprit is a computer virus, perhaps infiltrated into our computer but an infected email or download. A service provider's POS can similarly become corrupted.

The virtue of honesty, for example, can erode to the point of scheming against the customer's best interests simply to make a bit more money. The virtue of caring can wither into expressions of impatience, sarcasm, and even anger directed against the customer.

Companies have several courses of action available to them once an employee's POS is shown to be corrupted by a virus, albeit a psychological or moral one. Often, the company acts swiftly to cut off the diseased branch so that it does not infect the entire tree of the enterprise. Employees at Disneylands around the world know that behaving rudely to park visitors will probably lead to quick termination.

Or the company may task its managers with the responsibility to work with the individual whose POS is showing signs of corruption. These difficult but vital conversations take place in the form of performance reviews, disciplinary counseling, and on-the-spot interventions when a customer is being ill-served. Finally, individuals themselves can take time out for a necessary and regular review and possible debugging of their own POS. Such self-reflection asks questions such these:

•   Am I treating customers the way I would wish to be treated?

•   Am I extending myself by my constructive actions to show that my concern for customers is not mere lip service?

•   Am I moving forward or slipping backward in my attitudes and behaviors toward the people I serve?

The focus on POS is not merely outward to one's client base. Every company culture or habitat depends on healthy internal relations among employees at all levels. These relations, in turn, rely on the POS operative at the deepest level within each employee, from the most senior leader to the newest entry-level worker.

A case in point is Robert McNamara's period as leader of the World Bank. To demonstrate his complete commitment to his job, he made it a practice to come into the office on Saturdays not only to finish up work left over from the week but especially to get to know his employees. Because the leader showed up on Saturdays, many employees voluntarily took this opportunity to stop by the office to "chat with boss."

In effect, all involved in this kind of interaction were getting to know (and show) the POS that ideally would characterize World Bank operations and services at their highest level. When McNamara left his leadership position at the World Bank to assume other responsibilities, his replacement never showed up on Saturdays. Consequently, the workforce too gave up this valuable opportunity to occasionally take time to get to know one another and compare (in both conscious and subconscious ways) how their individual POS qualities measured upon against one another's as well as the standards set by the organization.

25 Principles of Service Leadership

Commentary:

Just as your computer has a Disk Operating System (DOS), so we all bring to our professional and personal lives a Personal Operating System (POS). Like DOS on the computer, our Personal Operating System usually operates in the background of our consciousness. It dictates how we perceive information, how we process it, how we evaluate its importance, how we convey it accurately and honestly to others, and how we receive and use feedback in our relationships.

In a sense, our Personal Operating System is "who we are" individually at a deep level. When others speak about us and our reputation, it is usually our Personal Operating System to which they refer when they say "you can count on him" or "he's totally reliable" or "she's one of the most honest people I've ever met."

Returning for a moment to the computer DOS analogy, we have probably all had the experience of having our computer invaded by a virus at one time or another. That virus was particularly dangerous to our computing if it lodged deeply within the DOS portion of our computer's Central Processing Unit (CPU).

25 Principles of Service Leadership

The result was often disastrous for our computing output: our documents were obliterated or filled with errors, our spreadsheets were corrupted with incorrect formulas, and our graphics were spoiled by mixed-up pixels.

Moral viruses can attack and corrupt our Personal Operating System, with a similarly devastating result. It's one thing to have a "bad habit" at a surface level—something that can be quickly corrected as soon as someone calls it to our attention. But it's quite another matter to have a moral virus strike to the heart of our Personal Operating System, where it lodges in a cancerous way that can't easily be plucked out.

An example of such POS corruption is moral turpitude on the part of a company leader. No matter how skilled he or she is in her specific job duties, a lapse into substance abuse, sexual harassment, or wrongful financial dealings can be an express elevator straight down from the executive suite to the corporate basement, and sometimes straight to jail. When such events occur (as they do all too frequently in today's professional and government life), the average person wonders "how could he risk all his success by such outrageous behavior?"

25 Principles of Service Leadership

The answer to that question no doubt differs from case to case, but has in common this truth: the erring person has left himself open and unguarded to the intrusion of moral viruses that corrupt virtually all "outputs" of his professional life. He can no longer be trusted; he has given up his sense of fair play; he has shown a lack of respect for his family, work associates, friends, and himself; and his caring extends only to himself, his own ambitions, and fleeting pleasures.

Many companies sell software to guard our computers against the hundreds of viruses waiting to strike from the Internet and elsewhere. We have no such variety of bona fide programs to protect our Personal Operating Systems from virus attacks. The best each of us can do is to be on guard against the first pinch of conscience that lets us know a virus is attempting to penetrate deeper into our nature or POS.

For example, if we find ourselves telling a white lie such as "the computers are down today" to explain why we haven't finished a particular report, the pinch of conscience over this prevarication should alert us to a virus attack. Our integrity and honesty in a small way is being challenged by a virus, and we need to fight back (as the immune system in our bodies does) by surrounding the virus with elements of our better nature and choking it out.

In the case of the late report, we can choose to tell the truth: "It has taken me longer than I anticipated, but I will have it completed first thing tomorrow morning." While such truths may be difficult to utter at the time, they are infinitely preferable to the slippery slope of using virus-like lies in increasingly greater doses to maintain our "image" and avoid the actual truth of our circumstances.

The battle to maintain noble motives, caring relationships, sincere interactions, and truthful communications is lifelong for each of us—and is one of the most valuable and courageous activities we each undertake.

Principle 13: The Principle of Personal Brand

The Concept:

When we think of a brand, probably most of us first think of a product that has been memorably branded by its look or qualities: a particular brand of soup (including the can of tomato soup painted by Andy Warhol), a detergent, or an automobile. Few of us think of people as being branded, and fewer still have made the effort to consciously establish a brand for themselves.

Why bother with branding yourself? In the same way that products like Coke attempt to overcome the "noise" of extreme competition by creating a impactful brand in the customer's mind, so people in all professionals and at all levels of service can advantageously brand themselves by

• Examining their personal attributes and qualities as seen by the outside world

• Seeking to fill gaps that appear when those attributes and qualities are measured against the expectations of clients

•   Practicing the demonstration of one's brand regularly and in varied situations.

Here's an example of personal branding. Richard, 26 years old, is just beginning his first serious career commitment as an accountant to small businesses. On the one hand, he recognizes that most of the small business owners who use his services dress very casually, since they often have to "wear many hats" at their shops and offices.

Richard, however, decides on an exterior personal brand reflected in his impeccable dress—as business-like and impressive as any Big Four accountant. Richard does so not because he loves to spend money on expensive clothes, but because he wants his small business owners to look upon him as the consummate professional—someone who has succeeded in his profession and serve their accounting needs at the highest level.

But external branding through dress, grooming, and keeping in shape is only part of Richard's branding task, and in fact the less important part. More crucial is the brand of attributes and qualities he embodies as someone who can be trusted with the most private financial details, plans, and problems. To give shape to this internal brand, Richard practices his skills as a good listener, a confidant who does not share clients' information with others, and a man whose professional advice is always focused on what is best for the client, not what is best for Richard.

This internal brand sometimes shows up in Richard's conversations with clients, but more often it appears in his actions. Richard understands that to be trusted, he must not only "talk a good game," but must follow through by delivering service that aligns with the values he has chosen for his personal brand.

For purposes of comparison, consider Richard's competitor, Sean. This man, also an accountant, believes that his clientele will respond to a brand emphasizing too-good-to-be-true deals, fast bucks, and supposed once-in-a-lifetime opportunities. Consequently, Sean creates a personal brand calculated to attract clients who are financially gullible, sometimes less than honest themselves, and always on the lookout for a deal, however shady.

Although Sean does attract his share of customers at first, in the long run Richard attains the sustained success he desires because his brand engenders trust—which, in turn, leads to great word-of-mouth advertising, an ever-expanding customer base, and repeat business.

25 Principles of Service Leadership

It is important, of course, to keep in mind the overall brand images established by one's organization in fashioning a personal brand. If, for example, you work for a company that emphasizes friendly, casual relationships with its clients, it would be foolish to brand oneself as an aloof expert in a three-piece suit.

Aligning one's personal brand with the organization's overall brand sometimes involves a crisis of conscience, if one discovers that his or her deepest beliefs and attitudes conflict directly with positions advertised in word, deed, and product by the organization. In such cases, it is often best to seek another employer rather than trying to bend one's moral and ethical nature (or internal brand) to the breaking point in any effort to mimic the company brand. It is also possible to stick to one's internal brand without compromise, acting as a change agent within an organization that needs to reform its brand in the eyes of the public. This kind of renaissance frequently happens when a new CEO takes the helm and lets every employee know that "a new sheriff is in town" with a personal brand intended to change the organization from top to bottom.

25 Principles of Service Leadership

Commentary:

Have you thought of metaphorically incorporating yourself? As a mental exercise, imagine "Me, Inc." How would you organize yourself as a business enterprise? So much would have to be considered: what would be your primary products or services? How would you brand those offerings? What image would you convey to the public? By what means would you market your offerings?

Just as important, what internal "rules" or personal policies would you have for taking care of yourself (you're the company!) and relating successfully to others? How would you apply your personal code of ethics to your professional dealings? How would you not merely intend to care about your customers, but actually show them that you care? What "feelers" or sensors would you put out into your environment to let you know areas in which you were succeeding or failing as Me, Inc.? What alliances would you strike to help you on your way, and which would you avoid?

This, of course, is not merely a mental exercise. It is the task given to each of us as we accept the frequent advice to "manage our careers first" and not place all our trust in possible rewards in the future for companies and organizations that employ us. The reality of "Me, Inc." emphasizes that we each stand on our own two professional feet and must be prepared at any time—certainly the ups and downs of the present global economy makes this point—to state the value proposition that we individually represent to others.

This representation may come in the form of applying for a new corporate job or by an entrepreneurial venture. In either case, we are gathering the attributes of "Me, Inc." and showing others how they can profit by linking up with our set of character traits, skills, initiative, and gung-ho spirit.

Principle 14: The Principle of Relationship

The Concept:

When we think of relationships, we probably first call to mind our bonds with family and friends. Although these relationships may have their bumps over time, we are generally grateful for the steady, unconditional acceptance and love we find in these close ties.

Can we expect client relationships to be comparable to those with family and friends? Yes and no. We cannot anticipate that every last client will look upon us as a brother or sister. That burden of relationship-building would be unrealistic; we can't achieve it and, in fact, our clients probably don't desire it. But we can use the same sensitivity to relationships with clients that we practice with our friends and family. In other words, we can have our antenna out no less for the feelings and attitudes of our clients as we do for those we love.

The recent term for this sort of sensitivity is Emotional Intelligence, or EQ. Much has been written about how to encourage Emotional Intelligence among organizational leaders as well as the general workforce. Companies as diverse as General Motors, Johnson & Johnson, Lockheed Martin, and PriceWaterhouse Coopers all have employee training programs geared toward improving skills in Emotional Intelligence.

But EQ means little without a simultaneous focus on CQ, or Character Intelligence (or "Quotient."). EQ, after all, is focused outward as an impression-gathering tool to understand the feelings of others. But is it enough in service leadership activities simply to be sensitized to how others feel? In the wrong hands—that is, in the hands of a personal low character—that knowledge of others' deepest feelings could be turned to disastrous ends, as in the case of Hitler's manipulation of the feelings of the German people in a time of economic stress and confusion.

CQ makes EQ meaningful. A person who has forged do a dependable moral base can be trusted with the deep feelings of others via EQ. An optimal professional relationship, in fact, depends upon knowing what to do with emotional disclosure; an inadequately developed degree of Character Intelligence (CQ) would tend to use emotional information manipulatively. In short, emotional sensitivity without moral maturity is dangerous in a service relationship.

25 Principles of Service Leadership

Commentary:

In describing service, the word "transaction" often appears. It unfortunately conveys the sense of a "one-time" encounter, or at best an infrequent occasion, such as the transaction of buying a new car every few years.

Service, in fact, is made up of an almost infinite series of transactions, few of them discrete in nature but rather overlapping both in time sequence and substance. For example, the transactions taking place between a psychologist giving mental health services to a patient can't be characterized as individual sentences said by either the psychologist or patient. Instead, all these interactions flow together into what can best be described as a service relationship.

Unlike the word "transaction," the word "relationship" connotes an ongoing context of mutual contact as well as a "give and take" from both parties in the relationship. Our idea of "service" can profit from these connotations drawn from the word "relationship." Too often, service is perceived something given to a recipient rather than a bond in which both parties participate. It may be fairly asked,

25 Principles of Service Leadership

"What does a dinner guest at a restaurant give to the waiter who serves her?"

If the service relationship is to be maximized in terms of its quality and likelihood of repetition, the dinner guest gives a great deal to the waiter: her courtesy (instead of treating the waiter as hardly worth her notice), her menu questions and preferences, her respect for the waiter's opinions, her expression of appreciation for service rendered, and her general demeanor of being comfortable to speak freely and cordially to waiter about the entire dining experience.

The result of this kind of two-way give-and-take of communication is a relationship—one that both parties look forward to perpetuating in the future. The woman dining guest will ask for her favorite waiter who, in turn, will give extra special service to one of his favorite restaurant guests.

Extended beyond restaurants, the goal of achieving an ongoing successful relationship is of far greater importance to service organizations than any number of individually successful transactions. Unfortunately, service organizations (take, for example, clothing stores) tend to train their employees on how to initiate, carry out, and conclude a successful sales transaction rather than how to establish, nurture, and maintain an ongoing service relationship with a customer.

As a consequence, in many business sectors customers say they make purchasing decisions almost exclusively on price point rather than on any history of service relationship with a particular company (often because there has been no service relationship established). Both parties tend to lose in this circumstance. The customer may find that price-point shopping does not give him or her access to valuable product or service information—and hence the "cheap buy" turns out to be the wrong buy.

The merchant, at the same time, loses out because his or her expertise goes unused, as customers flock to "big box" stores staffed (often) by minimum wage employees who know little about the products or services they sell, and even less about how to establish a customer relationship.

In such anonymous, "here's-my-credit-card" transactions, the last words spoken by the clerk are often "is there anything else I can help you with?" Although few customers actually say so, more than a few of us have been tempted to say, "Yes, you could help me feel that I've been served by someone who cares about whether this is the right product for my needs; who shows that care by knowing a great deal about the products or services being sold; and who expresses some willingness to follow up with me in the future if I experience any problems with the product or service I've sold. That's what you could help me with!"

The heart of excellent service is a healthy, mutually sustained relationship between the server and the person being served. To improve service, improve relationships.

Principle 15: The Principle of Service

The Concept:

Although I have used the word "principle" to describe individual aspects of service leadership, it is important to recognize that all principles discussed in this short book, and other principles as well, can be legitimately grouped under the concept of the mentality of service. This is a mind-set or what the Germans call a *Weltanschaung*—a world-view—that colors and gives context to all the principles, guidelines, and suggestions within its purview.

The mentality of service leadership can best be understood by contrasting it with the mentality of manufacturing leadership. The clear goal of the latter is to produce a product that satisfies market demand, including expectations of durability and quality. To achieve this goal, every manufacturing operation must establish and adhere to strict production guidelines.

Every aspect of the manufacturing process matters to the end result of a saleable product. Raw materials must meet certain specifications and price limitations. Fabrication and assembly lines must be designed for efficiency and monitored carefully for quality control. Even packaging has become a science for manufacturers, as they consider the customers' need to receive products without damage and ready for retail display in SKU-ready, theft-resistant packets.

The human side of the manufacturing mentality is similarly strict and rule-driven. An assembly-line worker, for example, is assigned particular tasks that must be performed meticulously and consistently, with a specified production quota expected each day. Manufacturing managers are no less constrained by rules: they must monitor all production processes and report accurately on such matters as recurring product flaws, production overruns, success in meeting deadlines, and employee adherence to work rules.

How different from the manufacturing mentality is the service mentality! The latter has no defined "product" to deliver other than customer satisfaction. Since every customer has somewhat different expectations for what constitutes excellent service, the mentality of service leadership can never be reduced to a series of strict rules. Instead, the service leader is constantly building relationships rather than forging products.

25 Principles of Service Leadership

One customer relationship may require frequent contact and "checking in" on customer needs, while another may be more casual, with contact on an "as needed" basis. Relationships are the heart and soul of service mentality, as can easily be demonstrated by calling to mind the "bedside manner" of a physician, the reputation for integrity of a lawyer, or the commitment to students of a teacher—all professions within the large tent of service leadership, and all dependent on the building of trustworthy relationships for their success.

Commentary:

During his many years as a professor in the U.S., Einstein was often confronted by enthusiastic graduate students claiming to have solved one or another of the problems related to Einstein's theories. "Ah," Einstein would say, "you have indeed found the answer, but only by making the question too small."

That's certainly the case with service. If we truly grasped the vast boundaries of the service sector in modern economies, we would be surprised—dumbfounded might be the better word—that our educational institutions and company training programs put so little planning, effort, or resources into teaching people how to succeed in the Service Economy.

Bear in mind, as mentioned earlier, that the vast majority of GDP in major commercial hubs and some entire countries springs from service sector revenue, not manufacturing. The old days when our sons and daughters could look forward to overseeing an assembly line are probably gone forever.

The new reality for those seeking careers now and in the years ahead lies in preparation for excelling in the Service Sector. That incredibly broad swatch of commerce includes virtually every occupation that does not make a product. It's easy to tick off a dozen service providers who may not immediately come to mind if your idea of "service" is restricted to restaurants and various other hospitality providers.

All the following make no product but earn their living based on their success in providing service: police and government officials at all levels; teachers; bankers and other financial professionals; most transportation workers, ranging from pilots to ship captains to train engineers; communication technicians who hook us up to cellphone, television, and Internet connections; ministers, priests, monks, rabbis, nuns, and other spiritual counselors; physicians and mental health professionals; lawyers; entertainers, whether "live" or broadcast in some way; and environmental workers, ranging from gardeners to tree trimmers to air and water inspectors.

Taken together, even this short list of service providers numbers into a billion or more workers worldwide. Significantly, most have received technical training, but relatively few have received indepth instruction and practice for the service dimensions of their careers.

So what? In almost all cases, their success in their careers depends more on their service acumen than on their technical skills. A teacher who can't relate well to students isn't going to last long in the classroom. A lawyer who alienates his or her clients will soon be out of business. A physician who is gruff with patients and has no "bedside manner" will find himself or herself working elsewhere, especially in our age when medical options are expanding and becoming more competitive.

The reasons why service has not received its due attention in educational institutions and company training programs have not been fully explored. Some colleges simply didn't know where to "place" a service curriculum with a traditional academic framework geared to the arts, sciences, law, and the manufacturing side of business.

Other programs struggled to locate the content of worthwhile service training: how do we train people to understand the importance of service and improve their service abilities? Still others felt that service training was somehow "beneath" them—the stuff that waiters and hotel workers should focus on, not highly paid professionals. (And of course nothing can be further from the truth, as confirmed by the many stories about socially obtuse educators and the thousands of jokes about manipulative or unethical lawyers.)

Principle 16: The Principle of Mentor-Follower

The Concept:

The master-apprentice relationship is one of the most common training arrangements in service professions simply because it works so well. Unlike regimented training classes or on-line testing, the master-apprentice relationship leaves room for questions ("Why did you do it that way?"), exceptions to general guidelines ("Here's our approach to this special customer"), experimentation ("Let's try it your way and see how it works out"), and modeling ("Watch me do it, then you try it.")

An ideal master is simultaneously patient and impatient with his (or her) apprentice. He knows that the apprentice has much to learn, and that many important lessons and skills cannot be learned overnight. Therefore, he demonstrates patience by letting the apprentice know that "failure" (or, better, less-than-excellent service skills) is a source of learning, not a "black mark" that cannot ever be erased.

25 Principles of Service Leadership

At the same time, the master lets the apprentice know when failures have occurred, and trains the apprentice to recognize potential failure before it occurs. After all, failure can only serve as a source of learning if it is brought out into the light of day to be examined, understood, and dissected. In this sense, a master may appear impatient to his apprentice. The master is always eager for the apprentice to succeed, but is equally on guard to point out missteps and errors that will lead the apprentice down the wrong path, perhaps to job termination if the problems are not pointed out and resolved.

At DHL, the master-apprentice relationship was a matter of covenant, not contract. That's a fancy way of saying that the master had a strong bond of responsibility and caring for the development of the apprentice (the "covenant"), but no legally binding document or legal framework creating boundaries around the nature of those obligations (as would be present in a contract).

Couriers themselves would describe the relationship in common-sense terms: an experienced courier with excellent customer relationship skills would take on responsibility for a new trainee, who would "shadow" the experienced courier and learn by doing. The process was characterized as "you watch me do it, I watch you do it, I give you feedback, you do it yourself." At all times, of course, the quality and efficiency of DHL's service had to be maintained and protected.

Hence, a trainee in his or her first few days on the job would probably do more observing of the experienced courier's methods rather than spreading his own wings to fly, so to speak. But as knowledge and trust grew between the pair of experienced and inexperienced employees, opportunities would emerge for small service steps on the part of the trainee that gradually turned into larger activities, all under the careful eye of the experienced courier.

The result was almost always successful. Trainees got to learn at their own pace while experienced couriers had the opportunity to pass along skills, techniques, and relational abilities that often were mastered over a period of years. The company thus made the most of its "knowledge base" (centered in its experienced employees) while growing its numbers of skilled employees to meet rapidly developing new markets.

The master-apprentice model of training has been called the "safety-net" approach to occupational instruction, since the trainee may "slip" from time to time in the learning process, but is always "caught" by the master before a mistake explodes into a episode that damages the company's reputation for excellent service at all times.

Commentary:

It's an old and probably over-rated saying that in most companies, 20 percent of the employees do 80 percent of the work. But, for purposes of understanding a mentor-follower relationship, let's take that statistic at its face worth. If a minority of the workforce knows how to do something well and the majority doesn't, the clear and apparent solution is to have those who know teach those who don't know.

This is the core logic behind popular mentor-follower training programs in global firms such as DHL, Marriott Corporation, and Johnson & Johnson.

The process typically works like this. An experienced, highly-regarded employee takes along a less experienced employee on a professional call or visit of some kind. The inexperienced employee is instructed simply to watch and pay attention as the experienced employee shows his or her skills in the art of providing service. This period of observation can be long or short, depending on the abilities of the inexperienced employee.

25 Principles of Service Leadership

There is always time available for questions and discussion: Why did you say this to the client? What do you think I should have said when he raised an objection? How did the presence of his secretary affect our visit? And so forth.

When the experienced employee judges that the inexperienced employee is ready to try out these observed skills, the experienced employee takes on the observer roles and lets the inexperienced employee try his or her wings. The results at first are rarely perfect, and several sessions of feedback and refinement are usually required during this second stage.

The cycle of learning is completed when the previously inexperienced employee becomes sufficiently skilled to take on an apprentice of his or her own. In this way, knowledge, skills, and attitudes are disseminated throughout the company, but without the stigma of branding inexperienced employees as inept or stupid.

Just the opposite is the more typical reaction: the inexperienced employee feels privileged to be learning first-hand from one of the more successful people in the company. Professional friendship emerge out of these learning partnerships that often last throughout careers.

From the company's point of view, the mentor-apprentice model works well because it does not pull inexperienced employees "off-line" for classroom instruction. Nor does it group inexperienced employees with one another, where they are as likely to pick up bad habits and attitudes as they are to learn higher level service skills.

Principle 17: The Principle of Historical Service Development

The Concept:

Long before human beings established production facilities, even in the crude form of sharpening stone points for their spears and arrows, they relied on service skills and service leadership for the very survival. Probably at first such service took the form of physical strength: a small human group was protected from predators by the muscle of its strongest and bravest members.

But service no doubt had a knowledge component as well as a physical aspect from its earliest days. The service leader within a human group was the person with a keen memory able to recall where water could be found during times of drought, where berries could be gathered (and which were safe to eat), and where shelter could be found or framed to see the group through the cold of winter.

Using knowledge on behalf of the welfare of others became the hallmark of service leadership from its earliest days. The tribal shaman claimed special knowledge to cure disease and ward off evil spirits (a tradition later formalized into the theologies and practices of the world's many religions).

The trader—Marco Polo comes to mind—used his knowledge of navigation routes to enrich cultures with new ideas as well as new baubles and beads. The tribal leader used his knowledge of basic principles of fairness to settle disputes within the group. Teachers, at first and still in the continuing roles of father and mother, imparted knowledge to their children to steer them toward life skills that supported survival and avoided fatal mistakes.

This quick series of snapshots is offered as a way of asserting that service leadership lies at the heart of our history and nature as human beings. No matter what our ethnicity or modern culture, we value those who provide needed service to us and we generally assign them high status: priests (by whatever title), police, soldiers, government leaders, physicians, teachers, lawyers, and so forth. We even recognize the service of waiters and hotel service providers by the token custom of a gratuity—something we don't typically give to someone who manufactures a product.

25 Principles of Service Leadership

Since the Industrial Revolution, however, the knowledge involved in conceiving of and delivering needed services has fallen into a prolonged period of inattention. Our schools, for example, tend to teach knowledge and skills that contribute more to the making and management of products (particularly in the wide varieties of math, science, and business courses) than to the building of trustworthy human relationships that undergird service in all its forms.

We are in danger of transitioning from *homo sapiens*—the "knowing human"—to *homo faciens*—"the making human." Only within the last decade have major educational institutions—notably tertiary schools in Hong Kong and elsewhere—recognized how dependent modern societies are on their service economies, and how ill-prepared its students are to enter service careers.

The principles contained in this short book are an effort to support the restoration of service knowledge and the encouragement of service education not only for traditional students but also for adult "life-long" learners in company and community training programs.

25 Principles of Service Leadership

Commentary:

Imagining life around a prehistoric campfire 100,000 years ago or more may be a stretch for most of us. At least from movies, the basic picture comes to mind: pieces of meat from the hunt being cooked over the fire, mothers clad in furs nursing their babies; our ape-like ancestors squatting close to the coals in an effort to ward off both the cold and possible attack by night-prowling predators.

Where in this Pleistocene scenario does the practice of service fit in? Wouldn't service to one another seem out of character for these seemingly crude cave dwellers?

Not at all. We can assume from the first records of human settlement that socialization was an important key to survival. Loners simply did not have the hunting prowess, defense network, or access to food and water necessary to survive.

Socialization, even in its first forms, presumes sufficient cessation of aggressive acts to hang together as a group or tribe. This is not to say that alpha individuals did not challenge one another for supremacy and mating rights. But such violence confrontations were apparently rare enough that they did not tear apart the social cohesion of the group. In short, there was "something else" at work beyond self-interest in binding individuals together as a mutually sustaining unit.

We can use the word "service" to name that "something else." Food brought back to camp by gatherers and hunters was distributed so that everyone ate—a form of service to one another. Night watchmen undoubtedly stood guard on a rotating basis over the rest of the group as they slept—again, a form of service. Mothers probably helped one another in ways large and small with child-raising—service of the most important kind.

Leaders emerged from amidst the group, partly no doubt as a display of strength and ego, but also to serve the interests of the group by promoting safety (the leader knows the best cave), hunting success (the leader is our shrewdest hunter), and even justice (the leader will decide tribal disputes). These roles were all patent examples of service to others.

It is therefore not overstatement to claim that service, including our individual impulse to serve and be served, are among the most primal of our early human experiences. There is every reason to believe that, like many aspects of early human life, the service impulse or sensitivity became hard-wired into the oldest portion of our brain—a portion that still guides our responses in many ways, many of them unconscious.

The almost universal pleasure we feel at being served well and the frustration or anger we feel at being served poorly may well stem from this age-old history, now our genetic inheritance, of service at the core of our humanity.

Principle 18: The Principle of Tradable and Non-tradable Service

The Concept:

It goes without saying that not all services are alike, and therefore not all service leadership can be described as a single set of skills, attitudes, or behaviors. One important watershed division in the area of services involves the difference between tradable and non-tradable services. A tradable service is any service that can be outsourced, cloned, "phoned in," or otherwise distanced from the receiver of that service.

Take, for example, the service rendered to a bank customer inquiring about a problem with her account. Although she picks up her telephone to call in London, it is likely that the serving "voice" at the other end of the call will be based in a phone center in, let's say, Calcutta. So that the London caller does not complain, "What, am I talking to India?", the bank has taken care to train those who receive calls from the UK to respond in a British accent.

25 Principles of Service Leadership

The service is "tradable" in the sense that its parts—
the location of call receiver, his or her accent, and
the content of the call itself—are interchangeable or
tradable. Other common examples of tradable
services are airline and hotel reservations, military
communications across continents, virtually all
Internet services, and many hiring and firing functions
in modern corporations.

What's wrong with tradable services? Nothing. In
many cases, they expedite services on a 24/7 basis
and make our business and personal lives easier.
Imagine, for example, having to drive down to the
telephone office to talk to a specific human being
every time you have a problem or other issue with
your phone.

But tradable services do create vulnerabilities. First,
the provider of a tradable service may find himself or
herself replaced on short notice, as is often the case
when massive phone banks change location from
one country to another based on cheaper labor
rates. Second, the quality of a tradable service is
difficult to fix "on-the-spot." Customers problems
communicated over the phone "may be monitored
for training purposes," as the common line goes, but
no supervisor ever breaks in to resolve an emerging
problem as it is occurring during a customer
complaint call.

25 Principles of Service Leadership

Third, tradable services tend to be rather aloof and anonymous. In many cases, those providing the service have a script in front of them (or memorized) that is said to all callers, no matter what the circumstances. A common script line, for example, used by those who serve complaints from computer purchasers is "Thank you for making us aware of this problem, and we are very sorry for your inconvenience. I will do everything I can to resolve the problem." If the customer repeats his or her complaint, the service provider repeats the script, and so forth. That experience of apparently insincere repetition on the part of the service provider can be maddening for the customer, who often feels like shouting, "Just get off your script and listen to what I'm telling you!"

Non-tradable services, by contrast, are those that happen "within arm's length" of the customer (or at least in real time with real people reacting moment-by-moment to what one another is saying or doing). A tradable service is, for example, a haircut—a "close encounter" with a service provider who is distinctly NOT located thousands of miles away or working from a script.

Especially in the world of women's hair styling, the industry would wither overnight if the service provider (the hairdresser) responded in conversation with scripted, robotic lines. Part of the experience of the female hair salon is the chat—the non-tradable service—that takes place as part of the experience. A nontradable experience has the advantage, first, of making the encounter more sincere. The service provider can adjust almost instantaneously to the needs, preferences, and expressions of the person receiving the service. Second, a nontradable service tends to be more flexible, since both parties are able to come up with compromises and other "fixes" that could never be predicted in a preformed script.

Finally, a nontradable service tends to yield a more stable, long-lasting career for the service provider. Once a relationship is built up with a customer through a nontradable bond of service, that union has value in itself, insofar as it produces further business, goodwill, and word-of-mouth advertising. For example, a person who has been well-served by the nontradable service of real estate agent is likely to tell many friends and acquaintances about the "great deal" the agent was able to negotiate. Any company employing such an agent would be foolish to try to out-source his activity in some way, since it would sacrifice the underlying value of the relationships that are fostering further business.

Where do we learn the skills of nontradable services? Not from company training programs teaching us to read a script or accent workshop teaching us to mimic London speech patterns. Instead, we learn them from our own relationships, first in the family with parents and siblings and later in our friendships. The whole panoply of relationship skills, ranging from direct eye contact to sympathetic facial expressions to active listening skills, are directly applicable to the world of nontradable service providers and service leaders.

In fact, one of the primary ways in which nontradable service leaders demonstrate their influence and expertise is to practice nontradable relationship-building skills upon those they supervise. A nontradable service leader would tend to meet a trainee for coffee to talk about "how things are going." A tradable service leader would tend to send an email to all employees instructing them on what to say and how to behave when they receive their next disgruntled customer call.

Commentary:

If I make a vase and sell it to you, I have participated in a tradable transaction. That is, you now have something of value that you can, if you wish, sell to someone else.

25 Principles of Service Leadership

Notice the crucial difference, however, when it comes to providing a service. Let's say that I am a banker and you are a bank customer. You enter the bank and I serve you with competence, character, and caring. I throw in a good measure of respect and fairness for good measure. You certainly can't exit the bank claiming that you have nothing from me; you undeniably have had good service. But what I have given you is non-tradable in the sense that you have nothing in your possession that you can literally trade with someone else.

Because we cannot use most service experiences to enrich our larder of tradable objects, we can value from them in other (and rather creative) ways. After you leave the bank, for example, it occurs to you that you now have valuable information or experience that can be passed along to your social and professional advantage to other people in your sphere of influence.

Even though you will not receive cash as you might in the case of selling a vase, you will nevertheless receive intangible but nonetheless real rewards in the form of another person's gratitude and perhaps even obligation, once you have told them about the excellent banking services they can find at your bank. Days later they may thank you profusely for your guidance in this matter—gratitude that in itself is a form of social payment.

25 Principles of Service Leadership

In an on-line age, much of the utility and popularity of social networks such as Facebook are due to the exchange of non-tradable service. On Facebook, we tell one another what movies we have enjoyed, what restaurants to try, what cruise lines to consider, and so forth. We turn "thumbs up" or "thumbs down" as a social community to indicate our general approval or disapproval of this advice.

On the flip side, we turn to on-line complaint services such as Yelp to warn one another against providers of poor service. All this information and advice has value—and in fact often can be translated into actual financial value in our own buying and selling habits.

Service, although non-tradable, has real value

25 Principles of Service Leadership

.

Principle 19: The Principle of a Service Mindset

The Concept:

Make no mistake: for all our talk about relationship-building and other supposedly "soft" skills, both those with a service mindset and those with a manufacturing mindset have similar financial endgames in mind—both want to see their efforts yield a decent profit after a transaction. The key difference is that the person coming from the manufacturing mindset wants the customer to be satisfied with product; the person coming from the service mindset wants the customer to be satisfied (preferably delighted) with the relationship and customer service associated with the service transaction.

I call the latter the "service mindset." While it is practiced, ideally, by everyone within the service organization, it constitutes a culture that emanates from the top of the organization and is carried out not only at the level but throughout the entire company structure. This means that janitors are expected to reflect "customer service" as surely as are salesmen, mid-level managers, and senior executives. In the same way that the student is (or should be) the focal point of a school, the customer is the central target of organizations with a service mindset.

When that target shifts or becomes fuzzy, service organizations find themselves serving their own internal interests, often in the name of "reorganization" or "operational efficiency," while ignoring the needs of their customer base. Getting back on the service leadership track can be difficult simply because it makes for an easier business day to ignore the changing needs of clients. "Business as usual" can become rote activity when the customer's interests are left out of the equation.

To keep that internal focus from becoming its only focus, companies like IBM often send their technical workers along with salespeople on customer calls so that these tech workers can hear firsthand the needs of the customer. As on IBM technician reported to us, "Hearing a customer tell us what he liked and didn't like about his IT installation made a big impression on me. I realized again what I knew and what the company taught us in our internal training: we are building systems to satisfy customers, not to satisfy our own curiosity or desire for technical experimentation."

25 Principles of Service Leadership

Commentary:

German psychologists in the early decades of the 20th century popularized the notion of "Gestalt"—an overall, complete picture or frame of reference for an experience, memory, or preconception. One's "Gestalt" of a situation, these psychologists pointed out, became in fact the mindset with which you approached similar situations, and significantly influenced how you behaved and felt in those latter situations.

What is the "service mindset"—the *a priori* set of assumptions (examined or unconscious)—with which we approach a service opportunity? I have argued already that the "I/Thou" mindset, in which a supposedly superior savior rescues a helpless victim, is ultimately unproductive in that it further disables the latter party and creates an illusion of power and moral elevation for the first party.

Nor can we seriously contend that it is possible to walk into a service situation as a *tabula rasa* (blank slate), totally devoid of assumptions and simply awaiting "whatever happens." We are all products of our experiences and can't entirely shut off the influence of those experiences in prejudging new circumstances. If I have been bitten by a bee, I will no doubt approach the next bee I see with caution (and perhaps a flyswatter.)

Since the heart of any service situation involves the development of a relationship, perhaps that's the best place to begin in suggesting a helpful "Gestalt" or mindset for new service opportunities. Relationships, I have suggested earlier, depend to a remarkable degree on the perception of caring.

The service mindset begins, then, with the mental reminder to demonstrate (but not fake) your feelings of caring for the person's needs. Listen empathetically, with frequent signs (a nod of the head, a murmur of the voice) to let the person know that you are following what they are saying carefully and with concern.

A final element of the service mindset is optimism. Your verbal and nonverbal communication can convey to the other person that you probably can help meet their needs and, if you can't, you will contact your resources to see what can be done.

We all sense and make judgments about a person's apparent mindset very early in any relationship. Once we have made up our minds that "he is cold" or "she is so negative" or "he thinks he's better than me," we tend to select aspects of the other person's behavior that substantiate our impressions. (We all like to be right!) It's all the more important, therefore, to be aware of the mindset with which you approach a service circumstance.

You can be sure that "your mindset is showing," no matter how you try to disguise it. Better, therefore, to carry forth a mindset that sets the stage for a good relationship, the resolution of needs, and the prospect of further business together.

The notion of an upbeat mindset and unshakable optimism is well conveyed by the story of two shoe salesmen sent to a Caribbean isle to market their company's new line of footwear. One salesman emailed his boss at the home office, "Prospects are terrible here. No one wears shoes." The other salesman also emailed the same boss: "Prospects are great here. No one wears shoes!"

25 Principles of Service Leadership

Principle 20: The Principle of Transformation and Inspiration

The Concept:

As made clear in Jim Collins' excellent book, *From Good to Great*, truly outstanding companies devote deep thought and consistent effort to achieving transformation of company systems and inspiration of company employees. Transformation is the planned corporate response to changing market conditions and opportunities. Agile companies are prepared to change any aspect of their business model that interferes with their customer-focused mission.

This willingness applies to even the most "sacred cows" of the company, including traditions begun by the founders themselves. As Collins himself could not have predicted at the time of the writing of his fine book, several highly-reputed companies described there have gone under since the time of publication. Analysts in many of these cases point to an inability or resistance to radical transformation as forces such as out-sourcing, robotics, Internet commerce, and unexpected global competition changed the landscape of their previous approach to business.

25 Principles of Service Leadership

If transformation is analogous to remodeling a car, inspiration is analogous to filling it with high-octane gasoline. Inspiration is an energizing spirit that communicates to the customer the company's commitment to meeting and, if possible, exceeding the customer's needs. An energized company shows in all its customer interactions and in its internal workings that it is enjoying the fulfillment of its mission. The old saying in sales has it that "when you're desperate, you can't make a single sale, but when you're at the top of your success, you are overwhelmed with sales opportunities."

What's the difference? In both of these states, the same person and the same set of essential skills are involved. Even the same amount of effort is present; in fact, greater effort may be spent in desperate times than when sales are brisk. The difference, in a word, is inspiration. The customer (whether external or internal) can see it in the person's eyes, bearing, words, and attitudes.

There's a "can-do" confidence that is contagious. People are attracted to such inspired individuals; they are enjoyable to be with and a pleasure to work with. Fewer obstacles to successful service relationships emerge because the inspired individual overpowers potential problems by a preponderance of optimism, creative options, and self-assurance.

25 Principles of Service Leadership

Whereas transformation most often arises from company-initiated self-study and re-engineering, inspiration can flare up on a grassroots level anywhere within an organization. Any individual can choose to come to work "on fire" for service to his or her customers rather than spending another lackluster day avoiding or ignoring what customers want. Inspired individuals spread their enthusiasm to their workgroup and, over time, to their entire company.

As these energized employees often relate, it's more satisfying to work in a high-energy, customer-inspired frame of mind. The business day passes quickly because work becomes more fun than cynicism or boredom. The high state of consciousness termed "Self-actualization" by Abraham Maslow in his Hierarchy of Needs occurs as we allow the inspiration we cherish in our private lives to also infiltrate and inform our professional lives.

Commentary:

Lao Tzu is credited with the saying, "Give a man a fish; feed him for a day. Teach a man to fish; feed him for a lifetime." The founder of Daoism is here commenting profoundly on an intrinsic problem with some forms of service: they seem to be short-term solutions to problems, no matter how well intended.

Lao Tzu is pointing out that the service of providing a hungry man with a fish is a solution not well attuned to the larger nature of the cosmos (Lao Tzu's habitual frame of reference). The cosmos favors those who can solve problems for themselves, not relying on the presence of enabling problem-solvers for their survival.

Put another way, Lao Tzu is impatient and discontented with any form of service that quickly leaves the party served right back in his original dilemma. Lao Tzu in this familiar saying hints at (and elsewhere teaches in detail) the necessity for a transformative kind of service—one in which the impulse and ability to provide service becomes contagious and scalable for those served.

In the specifics of Lao Tzu's famous example, the man giving the fish obviously knew how to catch fish and no doubt had the equipment to do so (a fishing pole). Lao Tzu urges the server in this case not to problem-solve in a temporary way by giving the fruits of his expertise, but by giving the expertise itself (the ability to catch fish).

Service leaders must bear in mind that what a service recipient claims to want ("a fish") may not be transformative in resolving that person's dilemma, nor will it be inspiring in showing that person how to help others experiencing similar hard times.

The NGO Viviendas Leon, which provides helpful services to an impoverished village outside Leon, Nicaragua, surveyed the village population to determine what they wanted from the NGO. Overwhelmingly, the most common answer was "food delivered each morning to my home." The director of Viviendas Leon assembled many of the villagers to a friendly social event at which he made a difficult but necessary speech: "We are not in the business of giving away food. Some organizations do that. We do not."

He went on to describe how his NGO could help the villagers establish a sewing cooperative, with the donation of a dozen sewing machines by Viviendas Leon, a bee-keeping operation for selling honey, and other enterprises. Those cooperative efforts, now seven years old, are a stunning success and have lifted the economic fortunes of villagers beyond their imagining. The villagers now make school uniforms for children throughout the area as well as a variety of other highly desirable and saleable clothes items.

The women and men who run the sewing cooperative are already making their own plans to start a second clothing factory, this time without donations from Viviendas Leon. Their life circumstances have been transformed, metaphorically, by receiving a fishing pole instead of the fish they thought they wanted. More important moving forward, they are now inspired to perpetuate the process of transformation by repeating it elsewhere in their region.

True service leadership attempts to forge transformative solutions to problems, with the goal of inspiring those served to become agents of transformation themselves.

Principle 21: The Principle of Global Extension of Service Relationships

The Concept:

In the twentieth century, the goal of most companies was to "go national" with operations and influence. Relatively few companies in the 1970s, for example, had the ambition, imagination, or resources to become a global giant. All that has changed in the twenty-first century. Fast-food companies such as McDonald's can be found in the every major trading nation and many minor ones. British department stores have opened outlets throughout North America, Europe, and Asia at the same time that companies from these continents have found profitable business opportunities in London, Manchester, and other centers of British commerce.

The global expansion of a product business is, in many ways, easier than the similar expansion of a service company. Marketing surveys and histories of similar product sales can tell a product-oriented firm whether they will have success outside their national borders. But products are usually not bound with "cultural baggage"—that is, products stand on their own as solutions to customers' needs without involving direct cultural interface with the manufacturing company.

A car produced in Korea can sell to a farmer in the U.S. Midwest who knows nothing of Korea or its people. He may not even know that the car comes from Korea. Price point, product performance, and appearance are all that matter to him.

The case is wholly different for service-oriented companies, as many have learned to their chagrin. For example, when Toyota established its first U.S. auto manufacturing plants, it imported its management style as well as its automated approach to auto production. Management is a service to those managed.

In the case of Toyota, many American workers found it difficult to adjust to the high-handed management approaches and behaviors that had worked quite well for Toyota in Japan. The company could not understand at first why employees were resistant to unchallenged authority of the Japanese manager. Why didn't American workers humbly accept orders the way their Japanese counterparts did?

25 Principles of Service Leadership

The answer lies in the power and purpose of culture that is wrapped intrinsically around the very core of service leadership at a global level. Throughout this book, we have emphasized the importance of understanding a customer's needs as a pre-condition to providing excellent service.

One of those needs, often unspoken, is cultural in nature. A customer expects, consciously or subconsciously, to receive service that is in harmony with his or her background and experience. Five- and six-star global hotel chains have learned that customer interactions with employees are different in Beijing compared, let's say, to Paris. Consequently, employees of these hotels have to be hired not only for the technical expertise (running front desk operations, for example), but also for their cultural sophistication. For example, they may need to have a sixth sense whether the customer desires extended "chat" (as might be common in a Texas hotel) or whether such casual conversation would be interpreted as impertinent, as might be concluded by a customer in Saudi Arabia.

Therefore, the global expansion of a service-oriented company inevitably involves shrewd hiring for cultural knowledge and/or in-depth employee training in the culture where they plan to work. Companies that ignore the cultural aspects of global service end up with local, negative impressions among customers as "that Chinese hotel" or "that Australian company" instead of "that great hotel" or excellent company.

Commentary:

In early tribal societies, trusting relationships were probably established one at a time. A woman, perhaps, needed to know that her young child would not be taken away from her by other tribe members. She goes to the tribal shaman, who pronounces that this child is hers alone and cannot be taken from her without grave punishment from a variety of deities. The woman tells her friend about her good luck with shaman. That friend, who also has a young child, goes to the shaman for a similar blessing of protection.

Flash forward 100,000 years. Relationships for global companies (and almost all Internet companies are de facto global companies) cannot hope to establish trust in the service relationships by actual one-to-one contact with their customers or other stakeholders. Here's where the power of narrative and story-telling comes to the aid of companies and other organizations seeking global reputation and relationships.

25 Principles of Service Leadership

In the same way that this short book is filled with mini-stories of excellent service, so companies use their media networks to send out "the word" where the actual event cannot go.

It is optimal, of course, when "the word" comes from a delighted customer rather than from an advertising agency paid by the company. The hotels most famous for their stellar service have gained that reputation not so much through attractive magazine ads or catchy slogans.

Rather, word of mouth from delighted guests has spread throughout the world, accompanied by the enthusiastic credibility that only first-hand experience can generate. These hotels regularly remind their employees that "our guests are our best salespeople," a spur that urges these employees to give their best service to such all-important contributors to the success of their enterprise.

The reputation for superb service can be extended globally, and organizations of all kinds should think beyond Madison Avenue in achieving that worldwide extension of "a great service experience."

25 Principles of Service Leadership

One way to create the kind of positive customer buzz that circles the world quickly is to provide service that far exceeds customer expectation. When the iPad2 was launched, a man ordered one on-line, only to return it to Apple Customer Service a few days later with a Post-It note that read, "Wife says No."

Customer service representatives decided to turn this apparent loss of business into a win for the company and the customer. They sent him back the iPad2 without any charge, this time with a Post-It note attached that read, "Apple says Yes!" That story, carried on major news services and posted in dozens of places on the Internet, has conservatively been read and enjoyed by millions of people.

For the cost of one iPad2, clever customer service representatives at Apple were able to generate a tidal wave of image enhancement, advertising, and customer good feelings for their firm and their newest product. Of course, Apple has not made this practice a regular part of their customer service program or corporate policy. Clever generosity in small doses, however, can have extraordinarily positive spin-off effects in terms of company culture, public perception, and bottomline sales.

Principle 22: The Principle of Habitat Management

The Concept:

So far we have described service leadership as a set of attributes located primarily in the minds of the service providers. In this chapter, we broaden that context to include a physical space—a habitat—that encourages all aspects of service leadership. A habitat is not necessarily a brick-and-mortar building, although many architects labor hard to influence people's perceptions and behaviors through the artful design of a business headquarters.

A habitat has been variously described by service leaders as their "home base," "mothership," or "comfort zone." It's where they go, literally or figuratively, to re-charge, discuss strategies, receive new information, share insights, orient newcomers, and learn from experts and senior, experienced employees.

Some global companies establish this kind of habitat through regular teleconferences that bring workers face-to-face in a private environment not shared by customers or competitors. Other companies keep their "hive" of international locations all part of one habitat by frequent visits from top company leaders and regular exchange of work teams across borders.

A habitat is characterized by constant monitoring to prevent viruses from corrupting the environment that sustains the inhabitants. The work of monitoring is the business of everyone in a healthful habitat, not just a single manager. Employee focus groups, computer-based suggestion boxes, a dependable whistle-blowing capacity, and a culture of "freedom-to-speak" across company hierarchies are all ways by which potential problems in the habitat can be caught in an early stage of contamination and remediated.

The power of a habitat to sustain and inspire its inhabitants can be demonstrated by taking a hard look at one-person businesses, often run out of a garage or home. Although these small operations may have the advantage of low overhead and high expertise, they typically lack the day-to-day relationships with other dedicated employees as found in a multi-member habitat.

Perhaps for this reason more than any other, one-person operations often go out of business within a year. There's no one to discuss successes or failures with. No one steps forward with advice on how to solve a problem or congratulations on a particular success. In short, one of the virtues of the habitat is that helps to satisfy our needs as social beings. Within the confines of a well-monitored habitat, we feel safe to share our doubts, ideas, fears, and experiences— that is, to learn from one another.

Commentary:

Service leaders take responsibility for the entire habitat of their service organization. The word 'habitat' stems from the natural world, referring particularly to a localized area containing all components necessary for the survival and perpetuation of the species it contains. In a business context, the habitat of a beauty salon would include not only an attractive and healthful physical environment (in term of cleanliness, light, air, and so forth) but also the social environment, in which employees did not make worklife uncomfortable for one another or for their clients, through gossip, bickering, and so forth.

This habitat would also include psychological factors, such as the management methods of the salon owner, as well as security factors, including health insurance, safe working conditions, and fair compensation.

A service leader often plays a key role in designing a work habitat; but his or her real work lies in monitoring and maintaining its health. Just as a habitat for fish can "turn" quickly due to pH fluctuations or improper filtering, so a work environment can be 'unhealthy' in terms of interpersonal relations among employees or poor relationships with clients. A service leader acts quickly in the circumstances to identify the problems in the habitat and resolve them.

The service leader knows in advance that the company 'grapevine,' the private communication that passes among employees, will not automatically let him know what's wrong with the habitat. Through unobtrusive conversations and observation the service leader can trouble-shoot the ailing environment without asking any one employee to be the "rat" who tattles to the boss on the other employees.

Since the employees are the first to be injured by a poor work habitat, the service leader works to develop a culture in which all members ("in the same boat together") consider themselves responsible for solving workplace problems. Some companies employ a third-party whistleblowing intermediary (usually accessed through an Internet link) so that employees can report problems without alienating themselves from the rest of the workforce.

25 Principles of Service Leadership

Principle 23: The Principle of the Diaspora Mindset

The Concept:

In previous publications, I have written about differences in "maritime cultures" (those whose history and traditions depended on the comings and goings of traders, whether by sea, air, or rail) and "continental cultures" (those who tended to build fixed manufacturing bases from which supply chains radiated and toward which resource sources were directed.)

Here I extend the definition of maritime cultures to include the "diaspora" phenomenon. The word 'diaspora' comes from the dispersal of the Jewish people after 7 AD, when the Roman Empire destroyed the temples in Jerusalem. The Jews were dispersed to Europe and Northern Africa and some even came to China.

This diaspora has since been experienced by various other nationalities. British nationals went to America, Australia, Canada, India, New Zealand and other countries. Chinese and Indians fanned out far and wide for the past two centuries.

In the process, China did not change significantly as a nation when compared to the major changes in the mentality of the Chinese and Indians that went overseas. The diaspora from China over the last 75 years has been continuous due largely to politics or ideology, while diaspora from India was driven over the past century because of over-population, in-country competition for work, and the desire to escape poverty.

Participating in a diaspora has a great impact on the individual who leaves a governing system. When these people went overseas they joined another culture. More importantly, no one from the old country could really tell them what to do because in their new location there often was no central ruling government. Those who originally went to America found themselves in the thirteen states, and it wasn't until later that they were governed by a federal government. In the case of the U.S., the American Constitution clearly defined what belonged to the government.

By contrast, the continental culture refers to countries like Japan, Korea, Germany, Russia under the Czar,

25 Principles of Service Leadership

Austria, Eastern Europe, and the Turkish, Roman, Prussian and Napoleonic empires. All those at one time or another had top-down systems of governance. Although these historical empires may have disappeared, the people's continental mentality remains. There is always the reflex to look to a central authority of some kind for approval or decision-making.

That reflexive mentality remains because, as Erich Fromm noted, some people prefer an existence of conformity rather than independent decision-making. Consequently, education and training in countries characterized by continental culture don't address the art of critical thinking or individual judgment. Lacking critical thinking skills and the confidence to use such skills, people in continental cultures attempt to meet complex challenges by reverting to a central authority for guidance or permission on how to proceed.

However, the core competency needed for those who participate in the phenomenon of diaspora is the ability to handle complex thoughts and systems without the reflexive need for authorization from a central authority (in effect, a "parent.") For example, when it comes to 5-star hotels, we see that they are from the diaspora nations, where the head or the owners of the enterprise are Jewish-, Chinese- or British-American.

Advertising agencies are all British and American; and business consultants are almost solely comprised of American and British. On the manufacturing side, the leaders are the Koreans, Japanese and Chinese. These, of course, are broad generalizations intended to make a point about the diaspora of workers, not to stigmatize any one nation or people.

Commentary:

In a maritime environment, trust must be so powerful that it sustains relationships over thousands of miles of distance. Merchants—some with all at stake—load their goods onto a ship that provides the service of taking them to a profitable market, often halfway around the world. Interestingly, this high degree of trust is usually not built up on the part of the merchants by personal contact with the ship captain or its crew.

Trust typically stems from the truth that "this ship has delivered the goods" before and is therefore likely to do again. Bonds of integrity similarly are earned by precedent: this crew didn't steal from my shipment last time, the captain collected the money he said he would and paid every cent to me, and I was charged no more than I agreed to for the shipping service.

25 Principles of Service Leadership

A maritime mindset is quick to give its trust to those who perform as advertised, but equally quick to withdraw trust and business from those who do not perform, show lack of integrity, or fail expectations in other ways.

For service companies seeking ongoing relationships with new clients, it is useful to expect a maritime mindset on the part of those new clients even when it does not exist. Assuming that you have "one strike and you're out" puts a premium on high levels of performance and creates a company culture that does not tolerate error—or repairs it quickly and quietly when it occurs, learning whatever lesson that error had to teach.

25 Principles of Service Leadership

Principle 24: The Principle of Anna Karenina

The Concept:

Leo Tolstoy in his famous novel *Anna Karenina* used the habitat of a family to describe a fascinating phenomenon: all happy families, he observed, are happy in approximately the same way, whereas unhappy families each have their own unique reasons and circumstances for being unhappy. In the specifics of the novel, Anna Karenina makes the unforgivable mistake, for her era and culture, of having an open affair discovered by her husband— an affair that ruins her both financially and socially, and some would say psychologically.

Tolstoy's genius has been extremely valuable in helping us discuss leadership and the service-oriented habitat. In Tolstoy's view, a family is a habitat; if everything there is managed and operated according to basic human values and constructive behaviors, and any negative traits within the family are not allowed to rise above an acceptable level, then the family will be happy.

However, in the unhappy family, the causes of that distress may number in the hundreds of factors. It just takes one of these negative family qualities, should it rise above the level of acceptability, to doom the family to unhappiness. For example, a gambling or drinking problem on the part of one family member can sink the entire family in a downward spiral of financial and emotional despair.

Tolstoy's insights took on new life in our time when Jared Diamond applied the Anna Karenina principle to the ecological development and domestication of animals. He also helped us see how companies are an ecosystem not unlike a family. In product-based companies, manufactured items must not violate the Anna Karenina principle by including flaws that rise above a level of acceptability.

In other words, successful product must pass the quality assurance monitoring of the company. Substandard products are quickly caught when the Six-Sigma System for Quality Control is applied consistently.

Applying the Anna Karenina principle to service leadership is far more complex and difficult than in a manufacturing context. Service, as described in this book, is co-created between the service provider and the service receiver. The intrusion of an unacceptable flaw, therefore, is somewhat out of the control of the service provider alone.

Especially in real-time services, there may not be an opportunity to predict or intercept an unacceptable, disastrous error. For example, it would be impractical to have a quality assurance team standing next to a hairdresser or beside a courier, reminding them of the highest principles of service and the consequences of an Anna Karenina-type mistake.

Given the susceptibility of service-oriented organizations to errors not of their own making, it is all the more important to recognize that one unacceptable negative trait or mistake is enough to sink the enterprise. For example, if a promised service delivery deadline is missed, the reputation of the courier and ultimately the company (if the error is repeated often) could be sabotaged without hope of recovery.

Because every instance of failure is to some extent unique, the service provider must rely on a robust, self-driven quality control system to monitor and respond to potential problems. In the case of a courier who fails to deliver a package by a specified deadline, the company may require the individual to supply a full report of the incident so that the customer can receive an apology and so that the organization can act to prevent such occurrences in the future.

Unfortunately, organizations often learn the importance of the Anna Karenina principle by experiencing its consequences. Take, for example, the extramarital affair between U.S. CIA Director David Petraeus and Paula Broadwell, his biographer. Once it was exposed by the FBI, no aspect of his otherwise superb resume could rescue him from resignation as the effective leader of one of America's leading organizations.

Commentary:

In Tolstoy's great novel by this name, Anna makes one ostensibly unforgivable error that causes her banishment from polite society and leads eventually to her suicide. The application to service leadership is as follows: one may do a thousand things right in building a service relationship or a service habitat, but it is equally important to avoid the isolated single act that will bring down the enterprise.

25 Principles of Service Leadership

U.S. space shuttles have struggled with this problem with regard to heat-shield tiles, each of which costs relatively little. Hundreds of millions of dollars of technology, not to mention astronaut lives, are at risk when a tile or two is missing during re-entry of a space shuttle through the atmosphere.

Service companies and their leaders should therefore think speculatively and intensely about the possible factors that alone or in combination could bring the organization down. Common among such factors is scandalous malfeasance or misbehavior by the company leader (a phenomenon that almost ended the presidency of Bill Clinton); failure of a product or service to the extent that people are gravely injured (recent contamination of pharmaceutical products); illegal acts by the organization itself, such as the avoidance of legal taxation; and gross negligence in the performance of a service (such as the capsizing of the cruise ship Concordia).

The Anna Karenina principle makes clear that no quantity of "good deeds" can make up for or prevent the consequences of one devastating error.

As a general rule, the literature on leadership practices available to business leaders and their employees makes the mistake of under-emphasizing

25 Principles of Service Leadership

"Anna Karenina moments" as teachable opportunities. For example, one of the most popular and influence books leadership, *The Leadership Challenge* by James Kouzes and Barry Posner, collects 19 desirable leadership traits volunteered by the thousands of practicing managers they have interviewed across industries over a period of 25 years.

As helpful as these traits have been in leadership training, they tilt the balance away from an equally helpful exercise: the careful review and analysis of "Anna Karenina moments" in organizational and professional life. Put bluntly, understanding all the things a leader can do right does not protect that leader, his or her organization, or the public from the consequences of a disastrous bad act.

Take, for example, the well-deserved reputation of Volkswagen over a period of decades for high-quality, stylish, and well-marketed products, as marked by the cleverness of the company's "Think Small" advertising campaign. Surely the amassed good deeds of Volkswagen, in terms of its management processes and public image, could not be endangered by an "Anna Karenina moment."

Not so. As set in motion by the stunning revelations in September, 2015, that emissions software in as many as 11 million diesel Volkswagen and Audi vehicles had been engineered to give false readings during inspections, the top leadership of the company was toppled along with the loss of many billions of dollars of company market value.

When this kind of "Anna Karenina moment" can have such a devastating and sudden impact on companies and its customers, any bona fide study of leadership practices must pay close attention not only to what leaders *should* do but also to the conditions that allow disastrous mistakes to occur and how those mistakes can be avoided.

In short, "Anna Karenina moments" in organizational life and in leaders' careers must be *studied* with the goal of understanding dependable monitoring, checks-and-balances systems, and quality control measures that can prevent such disasters. It has become a business mantra "not to be afraid to fail," but when failures do occur they are too often swept under the organizational carpet as embarrassments to be forgotten as soon as possible.

A better practice by far is to raise "Anna Karenina moments," whether committed by the company or its competitors, to high visibility as teachable opportunities for leaders at all levels within the organization. In this regard, we note that the world's major professions force their members to face up to possible "Anna Karenina moments." In medical practice, for example, the Hypocratic Oath warns physicians above all to "do no harm." The best hospitals empanel review committees to understand in depth what went wrong with undesirable outcomes of surgeries and other treatments. The goal of this kind of review is not primarily to place blame on individual doctors or nurses, but instead to make the organization *aware* of the problem and how it can be prevented in the future. Similarly, legal training reminds would-be lawyers to hold client communications in absolute confidence. Not to do so would certainly be an "Anna Karenina moment" in any lawyer's career.

In service industries, we must not shy away from "Anna Karenina moments" no matter how painful they are to discuss. The process should be frank and forward-looking: "Here's what happened. Here were the unfortunate results. Here's why it happened. Starting now, here's what we're going to do together to prevent a recurrence of this mistake." That kind of organizational attitude makes, as they say, a silk purse out of a sow's ear: a mistake becomes an opportunity for organizational learning and ultimate progress.

Principle 25: The Principle of Wrapped Service (The Hamburger Principle)

The Concept:

The Principle of Wrapped Service asserts that the vast majority of products are, in fact, only possible because they come 'wrapped' with services, many that customers may not ever see. What comes off the production line – the products that reach customers – are like the meat patty in a hamburger. The wrapped service is like the bun that covers the patty that people want to buy. The heart of a hamburger is really the hamburger patty, but a burger simply can't be a burger without the bun.

What goes into the 'bun' includes services like design, back-office functions, administration, logistics, marketing, retail staff, and all the other invisible services that support the product. No product exists by itself, although our attention is on the physical products we admire and are loyal to, be they our favorite smartphone, car, shoe or other brand.

There is, however, a growing appreciation of the services that help products reach us. These services are a major way of differentiating between one product and another. A strong example of a company that has invested enormously in delivering its products through great service is Apple.

Not only are Apple products created with careful attention to design, but the company has also gone to great lengths to design the service itself. Enter an Apple store and you will feel how unlike their store is, compared to most other retail shops out there.

All products are wrapped in service.

This insight is especially useful in understanding why some organizations are more competitive than others. For example, there are many countries that have dominated in manufacturing products but haven't been able to dominate in delivering global brands. The reason is partially because the quality of the 'bun' isn't there. In some cases, there are companies that are putting fantastic products together that fail to get off the ground – it's as if there was no bun to the burger!

This observation sheds an entirely new light on the omnipresent world of manufacturing and those involved in the making of products. Like chefs who are never allowed to peek out of the kitchen to observe restaurant guests enjoying the food they have prepared, too many men and women trained in product manufacturing have lost sight of their responsibility to the end user of that product—and the enjoyment as well as meaning that such a realization can have.

Throughout the world in less-than-ideal working conditions, men and women labor away for their entire lives fabricating products of all kinds. What goes on in their minds (and souls) as they work to keep up the pace of the production line and perform their particular task on the item being manufactured? For many, the overarching feeling during the work day is boredom. They fail to experience how the item they are helping to make is literally embedded with service—good things that it will do for real people once it exits the factory. These production workers don't make the connection between what's coming off the assembly line "why it matters" to the eventual user of those products.

Commentary:

The hamburger, thanks to the frenetic marking of multi-national firms such as Burger King and McDonald's, has become symbolic of an item "at the tipping point" between remaining just a product or blossoming into a manifestation of service. Put another way, cooked into every one of the billions of burgers sold around the world is the *potential* for the debut of memorable service, including the relationships, sense of self-worth, and motivation that comes with doing meaningful activity.

The idea of anything being embedded in your next hamburger may seem a bit strange—"I just bit down on a piece of embedded service!" But let's follow the stages of these wrapped and embedded services to appreciate their importance.

At its origin, someone is running a machine that shapes and packs the hamburger patties that will eventually be the heart of your fast-food meal. Does that person do his or her job in a cleanly, careful way? You hope so, because your enjoyment of your hamburger (not to mention your risk of food-borne illness) depends on this person's character, sense of purpose, and pride in doing the job well. In short, this important person needs to glimpse *the service he or she is providing to you* even in the act of generating the product that goes between the buns.

Next on your hamburger's path to your mouth is probably a jet, truck, or train. Again, men and women involved in the shipping aspects of the hamburger's components cannot be deaf, dumb, and blind to how their work will affect your experience of the hamburger. If they ignore your need for their on-time and at-temperature work, the potential service embedded in the product fails completely.

Then come the important preparation of the hamburger at the fast-food restaurant of your choice. Especially because this operation is usually hidden from the public (you may not be able to see the kitchen), you *definitely* hope that kitchen staff understand your needs and support their side of the wrapped service for the patties they are flipping on the grill. Such matters as the workers' personal hygiene, their ability to keep cooking tools clean, and their skill in cooking the patty so that it is neither burned or underdone as all important aspects of the service you expected.

But the hamburger does not leap from the stove to your tray. You spend a moment surveying the menu choices, all colorfully displayed to attract your attention and whet your appetite.

You step up to the counter, perhaps after waiting in a line of other customers, for one of the last and most

25 Principles of Service Leadership

important aspects of embedded service—your experience with the man or woman taking your order and delivering your food. As described in the previous principles, this interaction can be efficient and friendly, with due care for the product being delivered to you—or it can be slow, discourteous, and downright sloppy. The product carries with it the potential for excellence at each stage of its journey to you.

Although fast-food workers have received training in their specific job duties, it's a fair bet that they have never heard of the wrapped services in the products they are selling you.

I conclude by asking you to imagine a world beyond fast-food where every worker, whether in production- or service-based careers, appreciates and acts upon the potential for excellent service in every professional activity they undertake.

Imagine a world where "things *matter*" to people in producing the energy and motive to care about their jobs and the clientele (you and me!) affected by those jobs.

25 Principles of Service Leadership

This kind of world is not a pipe dream. We have all glimpsed it in occasional, perhaps frequent, experiences of superb service that cause us to respond with a sincere "Thank you!" and carry away a favorable impression of the employee, the particular establishment or enterprise, and perhaps the entire corporation.

There's no better place to encourage such service leadership than in our schools and in on-the-job training, where well-defined, effective curricula still awaits widespread development. If we all recognized and responded to the importance of service—including service-embedded products—in the modern world, we would reshape for the better our daily relationships, standards of living, business environments, and our expectations from governments.

It is our hope that this tour of the 25 Principles of Service Leadership will ignite the passion for professional improvement by educators, students, and workers at all levels. The quality of service we give to one another is indeed the key to our individual success and, in large part, to our professional happiness.

25 Principles of Service Leadership

Resources for Further Learning in Service Leadership

RECENT BOOKS

Adams, J. Stacy. Interviewing Procedures. University of North Carolina Press, 2011.

Arbinger Institute. Leadership and Self-Deception. Berrett-Koehler, 2010.

Armstrong, Sharon. The Essential HR Handbook. Career Press, 2008.

Badaracco, Joseph. Questions of Character: Illuminating the Heart of Leadership through Literature. Harvard Business Press, 2006.

Baumeister, Roy. Advanced Social Psychology: the State of the Science. Oxford University Press, 2010.

Behan, Beverly. Great Companies Deserve Great Boards. Palgrave Macmillan, 2011.

Bell, Arthur and Dayle Smith. Management Communication, 3e. Wiley, 2011

Bell, Arthur and Dayle Smith. Winning with Difficult People, 3e. Barnes and Noble, 2010.

Bell, Arthur. You Can't Talk to Me That Way! Stopping Toxic Language in the Workplace. Career Press, 2009.

25 Principles of Service Leadership

Bell, Arthur and Dayle Smith. Developing Leadership Abilities, 3e. Prentice Hall, 2011.

Bennis, Warren. On Becoming a Leader. Basic Books, 2009.

Burns, James. Leadership. Harper, 2010.

Chen, Chao-Chuan et al. Leadership and Management in China: Philosophies, Theories, and Practices. Cambridge University Press, 2008.

Dent, Christopher. China, Japan, and Regional Leadership in East Asia. Edward Elgar, 2010.

Drucker, Peter. The Effective Executive: the Definitive Guide to Getting the Right Things Done. Harper, 2006.

Essany, Michael. Steve Jobs: Ten Lessons in Leadership. New Beginnings, 2012.

Finkelstein, Stanley. Why Smart Executives Fail. Portfolio Trade, 2004.

Fiorina, Carly. Tough Choices: a Memoir. Portfolio Trade, 2007.

Gad, Thomas et al. Managing Brand Me: How to Build Your Personal Brand. Pearson, 2002.

Gallo, Frank. Business Leadership in China. Wiley, 2011.

Goleman, Daniel. Primal Leadership: Learning to Lead with Emotional Intelligence. Harvard Business School Press, 2004.

25 Principles of Service Leadership

Goodwin, Davis. Team of Rivals. Simon & Schuster, 2006.

Greenleaf, Robert et al. Servant Leadership: a Journey into the Nature of Legitimate Power and Greatness. Paulist Press, 2002.

Gronfeldt, Svafa et al. Service Leadership: the Quest for Competive Advantage. Sage, 2005.

Hackman, Michael. Leadership: a Communication Perspective. Waveland Press, 2008.

Hamm, John. Unusually Excellent: The Necessary Nine Skills Required for the Practice of Great Leadership. Jossey-Bass, 2011.

Magretta, Joan. What Management Is: How it Works and Why it's Everyone's Business. Free Press, 2002.

Manning, Susan. Ethical Leadership in Human Services: a Multi-dimensional Approach. Allyn & Bacon, 2002.

Maxwell, John. The Five Levels of Leadership. Center Street, 2013.

Maxwell, John. The 21 Irrefutable Laws of Leadership. Nelson, 2007.

McGregor, Douglas. The Human Side of Enterprise. Annotated Edition. McGraw Hill, 2005.

Michelli, Joseph. Prescription for Excellence: Leadership Lessons for Creating a World Class Customer Experience. McGraw Hill, 2011.

25 Principles of Service Leadership

Morgan, Gareth. Images of Organizations. Sage, 2006.

Nir, Michael. Influence and Lead. CreateSpace Press, 2014.

Northouse, Peter. Leadership: Theory and Practice. Sage, 2009.

O'Toole, James. Good Business: Exercising Effective and Ethical Leadership. Routledge, 2010.

Rath, Tom. Strengths-Based Leadership. Gallup Press, 2009.

Rumelt, Richard. Good Strategy, Bad Strategy. Crown, 2011.

Sipe, James. Seven Pillars of Servant Leadership. Paulist Press, 2009.

Smith, Dayle et al. Why Should I? Ten Keys to Motivating People. Lexingford, 2010.

Tannen, Deborah. Talking from Nine to Five: Men and Women at Work. Morrow, 1995.

Van Watt, Montgomery. Dynamics of Leadership in Public Service. Sharpe, 2011.

Worthley, Brad. Outstanding Leadership in a Service Culture. Made for Success Press, 2008

25 Principles of Service Leadership

YOU-TUBE VIDEOS

More than 1000 clips on varieties of leadership can be called up on You-Tube. Especially recommended are the "TED Talks" on Leadership, under the following You-Tube searchwords:

Bob Davids: the Rarest Commodity is Leadership without Ego

Steve Denning: Leadership Storytelling

Drew Dudley: Everyday Leadership

Rosebeth Moss Kanter: Six Keys to Leading Positive Change

David Logan: Tribal Leadership

Anson MacLauchlan: Everyday Leadership can be Achieved by You

Stanley McChrystal: Listen, Learn . . . then Lead

John Maeda: How Art, Technology, and Design Inform Creative Leaders

Sheryl Sandburg: Why We Have Too Few Women Leaders

Simon Sinek: How the Great Leaders Inspire Action

25 Principles of Service Leadership

John Wooden: The Difference between Succeeding and Winning

Itay Talgam: Lead Like the Great Conductors

WEB-BASED ARTICLES AND OTHER RESOURCES

As of May 5, 2015, the following sites existed on the Web, and are highly recommended for your review. They can be called up most efficiently by using these searchwords:

Articles about Leadership & Management—HBS Working Knowledge

Articles on Leadership @ LeadershipNow

The Leadership Lessons of Nelson Mandela—BusinessWeek

Ten Common Leadership & Management Mistakes—Mind Tools

Robin Sharma Articles on Leadership

Toastmasters International—Leadership Articles

Creative Leadership Articles—THNK

Margaret Wheatley—Articles on Leadership

www.ingramcontent.com/pod-product-compliance
Lightning Source LLC
Chambersburg PA
CBHW060558210326
41519CB00014B/3507